Thoreau's Morning Work

H. *Daniel Peck*

THOREAU'S MORNING WORK Memory and

Perception in *A Week on the Concord and*

Merrimack Rivers, the Journal, and *Walden*

Yale University Press

New Haven / London

Designed by Nancy Ovedovitz and set in Simoncini
Garamond type by G&S Typesetters, Austin, Texas.
Printed in the United States of America by
BookCrafters, Inc., Chelsea, Michigan.

Library of Congress Cataloging-in-Publication Data
Peck, H. Daniel.
Thoreau's morning work : memory and perception in
A Week on the Concord and Merrimack Rivers, the
Journal, and Walden / H. Daniel Peck.
    p.   cm.
  Includes bibliographical references and index.
  ISBN 0–300–04823–8 (alk. paper)
  1. Thoreau, Henry David, 1817–1862—Criticism
and interpretation. 2. Perception in literature.
3. Memory in literature. I. Thoreau, Henry David,
1817–1862. II. Title.
PS3054.P4 1990
818'.309—dc20   90–36011
                            CIP

10   9   8   7   6   5   4   3   2   1

TO PAT

contents

≈≈≈

illustrations

≋

preface

≈≈≈

This is a study of Thoreau's two books and his Journal. My selection of texts does not depend upon regarding these as his most important works (though I believe they are); rather, it is based upon the fact that *A Week on the Concord and Merrimack Rivers* and *Walden,* the only works that Thoreau conceived and brought to conclusion *as* books, bear a distinctively important relation to each other and to the work whose twenty-four-year composition overarches their development. My method may be called one of triangulation; through it, I hope to define certain deep imaginative structures that belong not only to these works but to Thoreau's work as a whole.

The relation between Thoreau's books and his Journal that concerns me is not one of influence or derivation in the usual sense. The Journal was, of course, the source for many parts of both *A Week* and *Walden;* it was the place where Thoreau first developed numerous passages that he later transferred into these books as he composed them. But the Journal itself changes character during the period in which *A Week* and *Walden* were written and, I will argue, was itself influenced by them.

This is to see the Journal not merely as a workshop of ideas, but as a *work,* an integral body of writing that Thoreau himself understood in this way. Perry Miller took this position in 1958, and it has been supported in recent years by several other scholars and critics. But, for me, Miller and his heirs have defined the Journal's integrity too purely in formal terms. Though it certainly is, in some respects, "a deliberately constructed work of art," [1] the Journal has other, deeper levels of coherence that belong to the broad philosophical and epistemological purposes Thoreau had for it.

One effect of Miller's influence can be seen in contemporary critics' tendency to overemphasize the formal and procedural differences between the Journal and Thoreau's books, especially *Walden.* In its incremental development and its private, meditative form, according to this view, the Journal is Thoreau's most characteristic work, against which *Walden* appears as an anomaly. [2] I do not find this view convincing. *Walden,* for me, is neither the epitome of Thoreau's literary career (the traditional view) nor an anomaly. Rather, I see it as a pivotal work. It trails within it the issues of loss and remembrance that, earlier, had found prominent expression in *A Week.* At the same time, *Walden* reflects the rich discoveries of perception recorded in the Journal of the early 1850s and, in turn, prefigures the late Journal's consolidated spatial vision. Though I find important differences of textuality between the Journal and Thoreau's books, and draw attention to them, what concerns me more is the intertextuality of these works—the ways in which they may be considered as emergences one from another, and all of them from the larger project in which they participate.

This larger project I call "morning work." The phrase, of course, is from *Walden,* where it calls up wakefulness (morning) and deliberateness (work), implicitly setting these forth as the standards for efficacious human activity: "[W]hat should be man's *morning work* in this world?" (36). Certainly, this is one of *Walden*'s most important and searching questions, for the author and for his society. In this study, however, I elaborate Thoreau's phrase with meanings that go beyond his immediate context, and I believe he would approve (and implicitly warrants) such elaboration. As I develop the term, morning work is most significantly the work of memory and perception as these faculties conjoin to serve Thoreau's emerging vision of cosmos. I see memory and perception as Thoreau's two key, inextricably related activities of consciousness. The changing balance of their relation to one another in *A Week,* the Journal, and *Walden* can be said to define the unique literary character of each of these works.

Considerations of memory and perception in Thoreau inevitably draw me toward the issue of his modernity. I have approached this issue with caution, and do not wish to make greater claims for the writer in this regard than his work can sustain. But, especially in the Journal, powerful adumbrations of twentieth-century thought seem to me inescapably present. Thoreau is a writer who, because of a unique mixture of predilection and ideas, stands at the threshold of an objectivist, process-oriented philosophy, even though he did not fully comprehend the radical implications of his morning work.

During the long period of this short book's development, I was helped by several readers whom it is my pleasure here to thank. Patricia B. Wallace read chapters 1 and 2, as well as the first part of chapter 3, skillfully showing me how to economize the book's initial movement. Frank Bergon gave me valuable stylistic help with chapter 2.

Sherman Paul read the entire manuscript, in all its stages and versions, and as he did so, he thought the issues through with me. For his acutely perceptive observations and the extraordinary generosity with which they were rendered, I am deeply grateful.

I have a special debt to Elizabeth Hall Witherell, Editor-in-Chief of the Thoreau Edition, who provided me with indispensable materials and information. Her assistant, Scott M. Kenworthy, helped me check manuscript sources. I am grateful to Robert Parks, Curator of Autograph Manuscripts at the Pierpont Morgan Library, for his kindness in making available the illustration that appears in the Appendix.

For dedicated research and clerical assistance, I wish to thank
Jennifer A. Peck and the following former Vassar College students:
Elaine Imbriani, Bill Maurer, and Margaret Ntegeye. Christopher
Wallace played his part by listening patiently, on many occasions, to
newly formed passages of my prose.

The Vassar College Research Committee provided important resources and assistance to the project, and fellowships from the American Council of Learned Societies and the National Endowment for the
Humanities gave me time for work.

Those parts of chapters 1 and 2 that provide textual analysis of *A
Week on the Concord and Merrimack Rivers* (pp. 9–35) were first published in an article in *The Thoreau Quarterly* 16 (Summer/Fall 1984):
93–118. Other parts of those same chapters, as well as the initial portion
of chapter 3, appeared in different form as chapter 2 of *The Green
American Tradition: Essays and Poems for Sherman Paul,* ed. H. Daniel
Peck (Baton Rouge: Louisiana State University Press, 1989), 39–57.

abbreviations

≋

The Princeton University Press edition of Thoreau's Journal currently runs to three volumes, the third of which comes forward to August 1851: *Journal 1: 1837–1844,* ed. Elizabeth Hall Witherell et al. (1981); *Journal 2: 1842–1848,* ed. Robert Sattelmeyer (1984); and *Journal 3: 1848–1851,* ed. Robert Sattelmeyer, Mark R. Patterson, and William Rossi (1990; in press). All citations of these volumes, appearing parenthetically in the text, will be identified by *PJ,* with volume and page numbers following.

Toward publication of future volumes in this edition of the Journal, the Thoreau Textual Center has prepared typescripts of the Journal manuscript covering the period from August 1851 to mid-February 1854. Elizabeth Hall Witherell, Editor-in-Chief of the Thoreau Edition, has graciously allowed me to quote from these typescripts in cases where a passage falls within this period. For the convenience of the reader, I have included in parentheses following such quotations the location of the comparable passage in the 1906 edition of the Journal, *The Journal of Henry David Thoreau,* ed. Bradford Torrey and

Francis H. Allen (Boston: Houghton Mifflin, 1906), cited parenthetically as *J,* with volume and page numbers following.

For Journal passages written after mid-February 1854, I quote from the 1906 edition. Volume numbers for this edition refer to the independently numbered fourteen volumes of the Journal rather than to the numbering of the twenty-volume 1906 edition of Thoreau's complete works. Citations from other portions of the twenty-volume 1906 edition, *The Writings of Henry David Thoreau,* ed. Bradford Torrey and Francis H. Allen (Boston: Houghton Mifflin, 1906), are identified parenthetically as *W.* Abbreviations for other works are as follows:

C = *The Correspondence of Henry David Thoreau.* Ed. Walter Harding and Carl Bode. New York: New York University Press, 1958.

CC = Henry D. Thoreau. *Cape Cod.* Ed. Joseph J. Moldenhauer. Princeton: Princeton University Press, 1988.

CP = *Collected Poems of Henry Thoreau.* Enl. ed. Ed. Carl Bode. Baltimore: Johns Hopkins University Press, 1964.

CW = *The Collected Works of Ralph Waldo Emerson.* Ed. Alfred R. Ferguson et al. Cambridge, Mass.: Harvard University Press, 1971–. Four volumes to date.

EEM = Henry D. Thoreau. *Early Essays and Miscellanies.* Ed. Joseph J. Moldenhauer and Edwin Moser, with Alexander C. Kern. Princeton: Princeton University Press, 1975.

MW = Henry D. Thoreau. *The Maine Woods.* Ed. Joseph J. Moldenhauer. Princeton: Princeton University Press, 1974.

RP = Henry D. Thoreau. *Reform Papers.* Ed. Wendell Glick. Princeton: Princeton University Press, 1973.

Wa = Henry D. Thoreau. *Walden.* Ed. J. Lyndon Shanley. Princeton: Princeton University Press, 1971.

Wk = Henry D. Thoreau. *A Week on the Concord and Merrimack Rivers.* Ed. Carl F. Hovde, William L. Howarth, and Elizabeth Hall Witherell. Princeton: Princeton University Press, 1980.

PART 1
A WEEK ON THE CONCORD
AND MERRIMACK RIVERS

I can sometimes recall to mind the quality the immortality of my

youthful life—but in memory is the only relation to it.

—The Journal, June 11, 1851

one

~~~~~

KILLING
TIME

On January 8, 1842, the day his brother John began to experience the first symptoms of the virulent infection that would kill him three days later, Henry Thoreau was thinking of time. In his Journal, he asks meditatively: "Of what manner of stuff is the web of time wove—when these consecutive sounds called a strain of music can be wafted down through the centuries from Homer to me—And Homer have been conversant with that same unfathomable mystery and charm, which so newly tingles my ears.— These single strains—these melodious cadences which plainly proceed out of a very deep meaning—and a sustained soul are the interjections of God" (*PJ*, 1 : 361–62). The sense of mystery expressed here regarding time's continuity (its "music") and the intimacy thus afforded between Thoreau and voices of the ancient past are familiar; his Journal shows repeated expression of these sentiments from the time he began to keep it four years earlier in the autumn of 1837.[1]

Thoreau's Journal falls silent in the weeks immediately following John's death, and when we finally witness another extended meditation on the theme of time, it is clear that something profound has happened. On March 26, two and a half months after the most deeply felt loss Thoreau was to suffer, we find this:

> The wise will not be imposed on by wisdom— You can tell— but what do you know?
>
> I thank God that the cheapness which appears in time and the world—the trivialness of the whole scheme of things—is in my own cheap and trivial moment.
>
> I am time and the world.
>
> I assert no independence.
>
> In me are summer and winter—village life and commercial routine—Pestilence and famine and refreshing breezes—joy and sadness—life & death. How near is yesterday— How far tomorrow! I have seen nails which were driven before I was born. Why do they look old and rusty?—
>
> Why does not God make some mistake to show to us that time is a delusion. Why did I invent Time but to destroy it.
>
> Did you ever remember the moment when you was not mean?
>
> Is it not a satire—to say that life is organic?—
>
> Where is my heart gone—they say men cannot part with it and live.
>
> Are setting hens troubled with ennui Nature is very kind— does she let them reflect? These long march days setting on and on in the crevice of a hayloft with no active employment—
>
> Do setting hens sleep? [*PJ,* 1 : 392]

There is much here—especially the almost suicidal trivialization of the self—to suggest the acute oedipal guilt that psychoanalytic critics have posited as Thoreau's dominant response to his brother's death.[2] But I want to focus on the passage's figuration of time, so markedly different from that in the earlier entry. In both instances, the essential form is interrogative. But where the questions in the January 8 passage work toward a sense of appreciative wonder at time's continuity, here there is nothing of either appreciation or wonder. These responses have been replaced by confusion and anger, and the God characterized before by propitious "interjections" into the stream of time has been replaced by a deity who refuses to disclose the true nature of the temporal order. This covert God, as well as the passage's tense despair and its riddling, enigmatic forms of expression ("You can tell—but what do you know?"), may remind us more of Emily Dickinson than of the buoyant author of *Walden*. The questions—insistent, desperate, and deeply cynical—challenge all Thoreau's prior assumptions about natural process: "Is it not a satire—to say that life is organic?"

Yet while angry and assertive, these questions are not solely rhetorical. When Thoreau asks, "Why does not God make some mistake to show to us that time is a delusion," he is expressing his deepest wish that time, as the deliverer of his brother's death, should cease to have reality for him; he is asking that he should no longer have to live in time, to endure the experience of time. The strategy he has employed toward this end is to have killed time by containing it, by taking the entire temporal order—"summer and winter"—within himself.

But the manner of Thoreau's question also reveals his perplexity at the fact that, despite his willed sense of its unreality, time continues to beat out its inexorable rhythms, as if nothing had happened. We know that this same sense of perplexity had preoccupied him for at least a month before he wrote this passage, because on February 21 he had set down in his Journal a sentence whose conclusion is missing but whose meaning is unmistakable: "I feel as if years had been crowded into the last month [the period since John's death]—and yet the regularity of what we call time has been so far preserved as that I . . ." (*PJ*, 1 : 365). For all his desire to live entirely within his "own cheap and trivial moment," to retreat into a realm of pure consciousness, Thoreau could not ignore the sound of the world. This inability is, of course, a mark of his essential psychic health, closely related to the palpable sense of nature that gives a work such as *Walden* so much of its power.

But here Thoreau's awareness of that sound establishes a severely arhythmical relation between the time of consciousness and the world's time, and this in turn results in a profound sense of dislocation and isolation. As the question "Why did I invent Time but to destroy it?" reveals, he is anything but comfortable in his self-determined imperial role, which protects him from the independent force of time but does so at a terrible cost. The passage reveals Thoreau's awareness that he could not kill time without killing the body of the world and the sound of its heartbeat, as measured, for example, by the life-sustaining song of the cricket that pervades his Journal early and late,[3] or the celebrated sounds that are the title of Chapter Four of *Walden.*

By killing time, Thoreau has killed the vehicle of temporality in which the world and the self have their being and their relation; in this sense, he has committed suicide, as, indeed, at some level he had intended to—paradoxically alienating himself from the very world he has "contained." For this most grounded of writers, a man who depended utterly on the variety and otherness of the world to feed his imagination, here was an untenable position; the impossible alternatives it implies are suggested by the famous phrase from *Walden:* "As if you could kill time without injuring eternity" (8). The passage, in other words, shows Thoreau trapped deeply within a solipsism of his own making, resulting in a condition of severe psychological impasse.

The Journal passage of March 26, 1842, can thus be understood— and, in fact, is easily recognized—as a classic case of compensatory overempowerment, prompted by a crisis that has put the writer's relation to time and the world in doubt. But this overempowerment has a philosophical as well as a psychological dimension, for if we were to detach phrases such as "I am time and the world" and "In me are summer and winter" from their context, they would remind us of nothing so much as ideas expressed in Emerson's early essays, especially the essay "History" (1841). This work, published less than a year before John Thoreau's death, set forth the revolutionary proposition—derived in part from European romanticism—that "the whole of history is in one man" (*CW,* 2:3), and, like *Nature* (1836) before it, announced and celebrated the primacy of individual consciousness over the entire temporal order.

It is possible that the sentence in Thoreau's Journal passage, "I have seen nails which were driven before I was born," is an unconscious echoing of the following sentence in "History": "I have seen the first

monks and anchorets without crossing seas or centuries" (*CW,* 2 : 16).
But Emerson's claim to a visionary perception of the past is an unam-
biguously celebratory claim for the empowerment of consciousness
and part of his larger program for self-reliance. Thoreau's claim to
have seen nails driven before he was born, on the other hand, is immediately qualified by the troubled question, "Why do they look old and
rusty?" The past, which ought to have rendered itself freshly to his
eyes, is even in the instant of its perception found tarnished, since
everything within the field of Thoreau's vision—past and present—is
tarnished. The very cosmos is tarnished for him.

In fact, the way in which the question "Why do they look old and
rusty?" undercuts the previous sentence's claim for visionary reach is
characteristic of the entire passage, with its clearly established pattern
of assertion and withdrawal ("I am time and the world. I assert no independence"). This is the rhythm of radical empowerment and the
(necessary) reflexlike counterresponse of self-negation: I am everything, I am nothing. For this disciple of Emerson, at least in his moment of despair, there can be no great surge of Emersonian empowerment without immediate disempowerment and a virtual swamping of
the self in its self-created isolation. The passage can be read, then, as a
short-circuiting of the Emersonian idea of the self's centrality to time
and space. The speaker's killing of time is a gesture as pathological in
its self-destructiveness as is the smashing of the quadrant by Ahab—
another Emersonian figure who, in destroying the instrument that lo-
cates his temporal and spatial "position," takes self-reliance to its most
extreme, transcendental limits.

Thoreau, of course, is no Ahab, and the comparison underscores
the aberrational character of the Journal passage, whether it is viewed
in a psychological or a philosophical (Emersonian) context; the intensity of response belongs to the experience of mourning. Yet while the
passage's extremity, even hysteria, is unlike Thoreau, the basic tendency it expresses is not. Frederick Garber has described the characteristically undulating motion of Thoreau's redemptive imagination:
expansion outward to bring all of nature within the embracing reach

of consciousness, followed by periodic withdrawal.[4] The response
dramatized by the passage can be located at the extreme end (the place
where grief had taken him) of his imagination's polar movement, and
may be seen as a severely exaggerated expression of one of his most
characteristic tendencies.

It is also characteristic of Thoreau to have understood the crisis of
his brother's death as a breach in the temporal order and to have measured his grief according to his alienation from that order. As the initial passage we examined suggests, this writer—from the earliest stages
of his intellectual life—was deeply committed to establishing a personal relation to time and was habitually given to contemplating its
pleasing mystery. Sudden, inexplicable death broke this relation and
shook Thoreau's faith in the benign continuity of time's progression,
which was the very thing that made possible an intimate relation to the
past. Thus, his figuration of time as a continuum on which the self
might ride without hazard had been severely challenged, in something
of the same way that his relation to nature was later challenged by his
unnerving realization—on Mount Katahdin—of its frightening otherness (*MW*, 70–71).

The Journal entry of March 26, 1842, can thus be seen to bring Thoreau's essential problem of time into focus: how to contain its unpredictable and wayward fluctuations within the safe perimeter of consciousness, yet also to honor the independent rhythm of temporality in
which the self has its earthly being—how, in short, to keep time without killing it.

The most immediate effect of the crisis the passage records was to
give Thoreau's general and long-standing concern with time a decidedly elegiac tone and to cast time as the foe from whom he would have
to redeem his losses. His brother's death had alerted him to the possibility of permanent loss, to the possibility that the living world of love
and relation that constitutes the present could suddenly vanish without a trace. The long gestation of *A Week on the Concord and Merrimack Rivers* (1849) was certainly Thoreau's mourning work of the
1840s, and the Journal passage's mysterious hens "setting on and on"
signal the writer's incipient awareness, even in the immediate after-

math of his tragedy, that such gestation would be necessary—that he would have to kill time in this other, potentially more fruitful, sense.

≈≈≈≈≈

Late in the composition of his first book, Thoreau changed its title from *An Excursion on the Concord and Merrimack Rivers* to *A Week on the Concord and Merrimack Rivers,* thus shifting the emphasis from that of travel through space to a voyage in time. Whatever his motives for the change,[5] it points up the important fact that *A Week* is Thoreau's most insistently and explicitly temporal work. In its way, it is just as much a "daybook" as his Journal, which in several ways it can be said to replicate. Its title announces this, and its organization—with the days of the week for its chapter headings—enforces it. By contrast, *Walden's* temporal structuring is largely implicit; the slow turning of the seasons controls its deeper movement from far in the background of the text, while the surface organization is, for the most part, topical.

It is true that *A Week* digresses frequently from the day-by-day progress of the voyage, but reader response inevitably is guided by its strict calendar. Even in the midst of a long and complex digression such as the one on friendship, the reader remains aware that the sun eventually will set on "Wednesday," the chapter in which it appears. We might say that the digressions are atemporal whereas the descriptions of the voyage are temporal, so that one sense of time works against another in a contrapuntal relationship throughout the book. But the larger truth is that, even when we are deeply involved in one of the digressions, we remain aware that our textual field is a "day" that sooner or later will close and be followed by another. We never forget while reading "Wednesday" that "Thursday" is approaching, and as readers, therefore, we are from beginning to end—like Thoreau himself—implicated in the temporal process. *A Week's* perspective of voyaging upon rivers intensifies our awareness of this process, because it commands that we shall always be "passing by" ("passed" becomes "past" continuously), rather than settled in place as we are in *Walden.*

As the speaker of *A Week* views each of the shore's shifting scenes, the river (of time and consciousness) remains his continuous vantage point—the perspective to which his commitment must belong.

We tend to forget that Thoreau might have organized this book differently. He might have followed the less strict chronological ordering of other of his travel narratives, such as "Ktaadn, and the Maine Woods," which he was writing contemporaneously with *A Week*. The method of "Ktaadn" and the two other essays that eventually were to become (posthumously) *The Maine Woods* might be called that of temporal framing: three excursions into the Maine woods each defined by the outer limits of its chronology and, of course, by its geographical range. Such a loose, external boundary contrasts dramatically with *A Week*'s strict, internal ordering of time, which has the effect of bringing temporality forward as the book's central issue.*

The title and structure of *A Week,* then, anticipate the book's dominant temporality, but they also suggest the particular tone it establishes. Unlike the natural cycle of the seasons that structures *Walden,* a week is a purely human and therefore arbitrary measure of time. This is appropriate to the elegiac intentions of *A Week;* Thoreau made the voyage on which the narrative is based with his brother John in 1839. Completed almost ten years after the voyage, *A Week* honors an experience that through a mixture of planning and coincidence happened to occur in the final days of the summer of 1839, but can now be memorialized—given to memory—by fixing it in the human record as "a week."

John's death helps to explain what otherwise would be a perplexing mystery: why, in his first book, a young author should have given himself so much to the past, to memory, and to time itself. Time, as a di-

---

*It is true that the third and final part of *The Maine Woods,* "The Allegash and East Branch," is divided into sections headed by dates, but the temporal quality of this work is quite different from that of *A Week.* The very fact that these headings are *dates* ("Saturday, July 25," etc.), rather than the systematically organized and richly symbolic *days* of *A Week,* suggests the difference. That is, the divisions of "Allegash" are functional and informal, like those of a diary, and do not alter our basic sense of *The Maine Woods* as a book of loose chronological organization.

mension of loss, had taken Thoreau's brother from him, and to write their voyage from memory was to take that experience inside of himself, to in-scribe it. *A Week* is his attempt to immerse himself in the river of time in order to recover from time his greatest loss. As the primary agent of recovery, memory serves him as a bulwark against his pain: "I can recall to mind the stillest summer hours, in which the grasshopper sings over the mulleins, and there is a valor in that time the bare memory of which is armor that can laugh at any blow of fortune" (295–96).

The most interesting thing about *A Week*'s elegiac intention, however, is the degree to which it informs other aspects of the narrative. In "Tuesday," Thoreau writes, "Since our voyage the railroad on the bank has been extended, and there is now but little boating on the Merrimack. All kinds of produce and stores were formerly conveyed by water, but now nothing is carried up the stream." He continues, "The locks are fast wearing out, and will soon be impassable, and so in a few years there will be an end of boating on this river" (213).

Like John's death, the "end of boating on this river" is a fact to be lamented. The writer's remembrance of his brother, prompted by the occasion of narrating their voyage, informs this landscape with the imagery of loss. Great elegies, such as *Lycidas,* characteristically displace and generalize their grief in this way, and the insistently elegiac tone of the above passage and others like it shows how closely related Thoreau's personal and historical losses were for him. Moreover, as the following passage from "Friday" demonstrates, *A Week*'s sense of historical loss extends much deeper into the past than contemporary changes in navigation.

> Some have thought that the gales do not at present waft to the voyager the natural and original fragrance of the land, such as the early navigators described, and that the loss of many odoriferous native plants, sweet-scented grasses and medicinal herbs, which formerly sweetened the atmosphere, and rendered it salubrious, by the grazing of cattle and the rooting of swine, is the source of many diseases which now prevail. [355]

Like Fitzgerald's fresh, green breast of the new world, Thoreau's "original fragrance of the land" has been spoiled by time, and the narrator of
A Week wants to recover from time a lost world.

It should be noted at this point that while *A Week* is, for Thoreau,
peculiarly retrospective, the elegizing, memorializing dimension of his
work is not unique to this book. His mature Journal of the 1850s is a
profound attempt to "hold" experience, and *Walden,* for all its buoyancy, has its own deeply elegiac character. No less than Jack Kerouac,
another voyager of the Merrimack River, Thoreau should be thought
of as a "great rememberer."[6] This aspect of his work can be seen, in
part, as an expression of his and his generation's concern to recon-
struct the past in order to prove that America had a history; indeed,
this concern receives explicit attention in *A Week* (250). But, as I have
suggested, the power of Thoreau's elegiac vision has deeper sources.

A Week, then, should be considered an exemplary case of remembrance in Thoreau's work. Just how deeply retrospective a work it is
can be seen in its opening passages. Though the voyage gradually takes
on an authentic aspect of adventure (there is much in the book to suggest that Thoreau and his brother are playing primitive, identifying,
for example, with Robin Hood and with the "old voyageurs" [172]),
its first chapter has little of adventure in it. In "Concord River," Thoreau prepares us for the voyage not by anticipating its course but by
looking back toward the river's sources and its past.[7] The chapter's
concluding sentence expresses a reluctance to depart ("at last I resolved to launch myself" [13]), and as the brothers drift away from
Concord in "Saturday" we sense their difficulty in leaving behind "the
last of these familiar meadows" (21).

Eventually, of course, the voyage leaves Concord behind and takes
on a prospective character. Yet these voyagers are traveling forward in
order to get back,[8] and at every stage of their journey memory makes
itself powerfully felt. In "Saturday," for example, Thoreau writes, "I
can just remember an old brown-coated man who was the Walton of
this stream. . . . He was always to be seen in serene afternoons haunting the river." Thoreau reports that he was the sole witness of the old

man's final disappearance into "his low-roofed house in the skirts of
the village. I think nobody else saw him; nobody else remembers him
now, for he soon after died" (24–25). The guarded place the old man
reserves in Thoreau's memory suggests that his death is cognate with
that of the lost brother whose name is never mentioned in *A Week* but
who has many surrogates.

The relation of memory to mortality comes up again in "Saturday"
in connection with another fisherman of the Concord shore: "I can
faintly remember to have seen this same fisher in my earliest youth, still
as near the river as he could get, with uncertain undulatory step, after
so many things had gone down stream, swinging a scythe in the
meadow, . . . himself as yet not cut down by the Great Mower" (35).
This memory too, with its poignant reference to things that have gone
down stream, suggests Thoreau's deeper losses. But what needs to
concern us most in these passages about shadowy, Wordsworthian figures from the writer's youth is the way in which they dramatize the
struggle to remember. Thoreau can "just remember" the old brown-
coated man, and he can only "faintly remember" the other fisherman.
Both accounts, even as they communicate the power of personal memory, reveal its limits. They confirm that Thoreau, in his developing history of the rivers' life, will have to consult others whose memories extend deeper into the past than his, and at various points in *A Week* we
find him querying the inhabitants of the shore.

Just as Thoreau's own memories tell of loss, so too these inhabitants
very often describe a rupture between the worlds of past and present,
and communicate the sense of a shoreline despoiled by the passage of
time. In "Monday," for example, the brothers "passed a small desert"
on the east bank of the Merrimack between Tyngsborough and Hudson: "A very old inhabitant . . . told us that he remembered when corn
and grain grew there" (146). And in "Tuesday" they come upon "another extensive desert" in Litchfield, which "[t]hirty or forty years
ago, as we were told, . . . was a sheep pasture." The railroads, Thoreau
adds, have in recent times further eroded such "irritable districts,"
converting "fertile farms into deserts" (198, 199).

One of the most compelling testimonies of the shore's inhabitants comes from the Sudbury shore farmers, who in "Concord River" tell Thoreau "that thousands of acres are flooded now, since the dams have been erected, where they remember to have seen the white honey-suckle or clover growing once, and they could go dry with shoes only in summer. Now there is nothing but blue-joint and sedge and cut-grass there, standing in water all the year round" (6). Like the passage cited earlier lamenting the end of boating on the Concord, this one has a "then and now" structure characteristic of *A Week*. As before, the image it draws is one of devastation ("Now there is nothing") and dis-continuity caused by the intrusion of technology—in the first case by the railroad and in the second by the dam. We recognize in both in-stances, and in the passage above on the conversion of fertile farms into deserts, a familiar theme in Thoreau's work whose most famous image is that of the railroad cutting through the pastoral landscape of *Walden*.

But if the testimony of Thoreau's witnesses describes a discontinuity between the worlds of then and now, from another point of view their memories of lost worlds can be said to restore continuity. By remem-bering they provide images of plenitude and beauty that otherwise would have been irretrievably lost. The stories they tell about the past are essential acts of preservation, in very much the sense that Hannah Arendt intends when she says that remembrance through storytelling is a crucial vehicle for human continuity in the modern world.[9] As Thoreau joins his own memories to those of others, he and the book he is making (the composite story he is telling) create a new kind of continuity, a continuity of consciousness. In this way, remembering becomes redemptive.*

---

*The process is directly analogous to Thoreau's recovery of his own past. In "Tuesday," he recalls from his childhood in Concord the "fabulous rivermen" he saw "stealing mysteriously through the meadows" (211). Just as going to Walden Pond—"that fabulous landscape of my infant dreams" (*Wa*, 156)—enables the re-covery of an earlier (childhood) self, voyaging on the river opens the way for Tho-reau to become his own fabulous riverman, to recover his visions of childhood and give continuity to his experience by reliving them.

But the other side of remembering is forgetting, and if the farmers of the Sudbury shore carry in their memories an image of the landscape before the floods, *A Week* offers other instances in which no such memory exists. In "Friday," Thoreau turns to "the record of an old inhabitant of Tyngsboro', now dead, whose farm we were now gliding past." According to this record, "one of the greatest freshets on this river took place in October, 1785, and its height was marked by a nail driven into an apple-tree behind his house." Thoreau's account of his investigation of this site gives us an allegory dramatizing the potentially destructive consequences of forgetting. The mark in the apple tree referred to in the opening sentence is nothing less than a symbol for memory.

> One of his descendants has shown this to me, and I judged it to be at least seventeen or eighteen feet above the level of the river at the time. According to Barber, the river rose twenty-one feet above the common high-water mark, at Bradford in the year 1818. Before the Lowell and Nashua railroad was built, the engineer made inquiries of the inhabitants along the banks as to how high they had known the river to rise. When he came to this house he was conducted to the apple-tree, and as the nail was not then visible, the lady of the house placed her hand on the trunk *where she said that she remembered the nail to have been from her childhood.* In the meanwhile the old man put his arm inside the tree, which was hollow, and felt the point of the nail sticking through, and it was exactly opposite to her hand. The spot is now plainly marked by a notch in the bark. *But as no one else remembered* the river to have risen so high as this, the engineer disregarded this statement, and I learn that there has since been a freshet which rose within nine inches of the rails at Biscuit Brook, and such a freshet as that of 1785 would have covered the railroad two feet deep. [356; emphases added] [10]

The story of the disregarded mark in the apple tree adds still another dimension to our discussion, because unlike the flooding of the Sudbury meadows, which was described to Thoreau by living informants, the Tyngsborough flood of 1785 becomes known to him through the historical record. This suggests his dependence on sources that lie beyond the boundary of his own and others' living memories.

Thoreau usually turns with greater enthusiasm to the memories of the living than he does to the historical record, in part because he so highly values the immediacy and spontaneity of speech;[11] for him the "word that is written may be postponed, but not that on the lip" (*Wk,* 312). This is why, for example, he prizes the "piscatorial history" of the Concord River near Nashua that he has learned from a haymaker whose "memory and imagination were fertile in fishermen's tales of floating isles in bottomless ponds" (160). In *A Week,* Thoreau often evokes and celebrates oral culture, yet he is aware that in making his book he must translate such culture into writing and thus risk a diminishment of its life. In turn, he himself is dependent on the written records of others, if only because living speech, no matter how fertile, cannot render the rivers' more remote past. For this he must turn to historical documents (especially his gazetteer, which supplies him with the local history of sites along the river), and he does so frequently.

Thoreau's consultation of such documents, however, is often characterized by a deft and even ironic distancing from his source. Seeking to fill out his knowledge of the Concord meadows in the opening chapter, for example, he says, "Let us here read what old Johnson says of these meadows in his 'Wonder-working Providence,' which gives the account of New England from 1628 to 1652, and see how matters looked to him" (10). The sentence's casual opening as well as the unceremonious appellation immediately rob old Johnson's testimony of any privileged authority. And while the sentence's closing phrase shows Thoreau's respect for the Puritan historian's experience and his own desire to try to see what Johnson saw, it also makes clear that this view, like any single view, is partial. To make a claim for truth, it must be placed against other perspectives.

Thoreau's ambivalent treatment of Johnson's account is characteristic. He reads history in order to recover a sense of primary contact with the past, much like William Carlos Williams in *In the American Grain* (1925), yet he knows that the historian's vision is severely limited: "There are secret articles in our treaties with the gods, of more importance than all the rest, which the historian can never know" (*Wk*, 125). This distrust of the historian derives in part from Thoreau's belief, which he shares with Emerson, that history obstructs an original relation to the universe by supplanting the eternal with the merely transient. At various points throughout *A Week* he demotes history (usually in favor of "myth"), because what he wants is not a relation to time, which is limited, but to timelessness.[12]

But Thoreau's suspicion of the historian has a more immediate source. He is sensitive to the way in which the historical record, through self-serving distortion and omission, can destroy vital elements of the past. He feels this with special force in relation to the American settlers' treatment of the Indians. Recounting in "Monday" the Lovewell expedition's bloody battle with the Indians, he refers to "an old journal" that tells how two members of the company, both severely wounded and without provisions, managed to return home where they "lived many years in a crippled state to enjoy their pension. But alas! of the crippled Indians, and their adventures in the woods, . . . how many balls lodged with them, how it fared with their cranberries, what Berwick or Saco they got into, and finally what pension or township was granted them, there is no journal to tell" (121, 122).

The paucity of the Indian record is also a subject of Thoreau's musing in "Sunday" on the decayed village of Billerica. Now "in its dotage," with its "farms all run out, meeting-house grown gray and racked with age," its "early youth" is nevertheless preserved in "town records, old, tattered, time-worn, weather-stained chronicles, [which] contain the Indian sachem's mark perchance, an arrow or a beaver, and the few fatal words by which he deeded his hunting grounds away" (50, 53). Compared to the copious documentation of white settlement, evidence of the Indian presence is incomplete and fragmentary, and the reason for this of course is that the record has been created by whites. ("For Indian deeds," Thoreau writes in an 1842 Journal entry, "there must be an Indian memory—the white man will remember his own only" [*PJ*, 2 : 38–39].) The enormous power that writing confers upon the record-maker/historian is related, for Thoreau, to the larger power of conceptual thought, as his description of the settlement of Billerica makes clear: "The white man comes, pale as the dawn, with a load of thought, with a slumbering intelligence as a fire raked up, knowing well what he knows, not guessing but calculating; . . . building a house that endures [unlike that of the Indians], a framed house. He buys the Indian's moccasins and baskets, then buys his hunting-grounds, and at length forgets where he is buried, and ploughs up his bones" (53).

With their poignant evocation of a lost sacramental sense, the final phrases of this remarkable passage show how narrowly selective and therefore destructive the historical record has been; lacking a written history of their own, the Indians have in effect fallen out of human memory. Thoreau's massive research in his Indian Notebooks, as well as his lifelong search for arrowheads and other relics, suggest that he may have been preparing to write a book[13] whose purpose would have been to re-member the Indians, to put back together their shattered past and give them the history that white settlement had denied them. Had he written it, Thoreau would have wanted his Indian book to demonstrate that historical writing, like memory itself, could be re-demptive rather than destructive. And this idea in turn suggests that he will find existing historical documents useful in his reconstruction of the rivers' past exactly to the degree that he is able to appropriate them for the purposes of redemption.

The Indians have a special place in Thoreau's historical imagination because, as America's original inhabitants, they offer an ideal of simplicity against which all of civilization's destructive complexities can be measured. Claude Lévi-Strauss's image of the temporal flow of the West invading a timeless continent[14] corresponds closely to Thoreau's sense of what happened to pre-Columbian America. But if the Indians were history's first American victims, they were not its last. Other, later inhabitants of the river have also been displaced, such as the "now extinct" race of early nineteenth-century Concord River fisher-men about whom Thoreau "would like to know more." He writes, "But, alas, no record of these fishers' lives remains" (34, 35). The voy-age of *A Week* is an attempt to reclaim both the lost world of the Indians and that of these fishermen; its deep sense of historical loss applies to the whole reach of the rivers' past.

This redemptive purpose suggests the important relation between *A Week* and twentieth-century works such as Williams's *In the American Grain* and Charles Olson's *Maximus Poems* (1960–), which also attempt to reclaim a usable past. Like Williams and Olson, Thoreau addresses history as an artist who—through style—will appropriate its documents toward a creative reconstruction of the past. That is, he brings to history (the mere past) the vivifying, synthesizing power of personal memory, which is for him the present activity of (historical) imagination. As Olson puts it in *Maximus II,* "my memory is / the history of time." [15]

A Week's best and most sustained example of creative remembering is Thoreau's treatment in "Thursday" of the Hannah Duston captivity narrative.[16] This beautifully written set piece, added late in *A Week*'s composition, is different from the book's other narrations of Puritan-Indian history in that it begins without any preliminary references to its source in the historical record: "On the thirty-first day of March, one hundred and forty-two years before this, probably about this time in the afternoon, there were hurriedly paddling down this part of the river, between the pine woods which then fringed these banks, two white women and a boy, who had left an island at the mouth of the Contoocook before daybreak" (320).

The rest of the episode's long introductory paragraph renders its dramatic events in a calm, unhurried past tense whose tone is balanced between that of "history" and that of "story." Its careful pacing and its restraint are especially notable because the events it describes are so violent: Hannah's capture by the Indians, the dashing of her infant's brains against a tree, the long and arduous march to the Indian camp, Hannah's killing of her captors in their sleep, her escape upon the river with her companions, their return to the camp to take the Indians' scalps so as to prove the truth of their story, and, finally, their "retracing [of] their steps to the shore in the twilight, [where they] recommenced their voyage" (322).

With the first sentence of the second paragraph, the narration shifts abruptly into the present, as the historical time of Henry Thoreau and Hannah Duston suddenly conflate: "Early this morning this deed was performed, and now . . . these tired women and this boy . . . are making a hasty meal of parched corn and moose-meat, while their canoe glides under these pine roots whose stumps are still standing on the bank" (322). The stumps, which symbolize both temporal decay and continuity between past and present, are replaced by a "primeval forest [that] stretches away uninterrupted to Canada or to the 'South Sea'" (323). The second paragraph sustains the present tense throughout, creating the effect that Thoreau and his brother John have joined Hannah's party and are participating in its flight.

This convergence, however, is too precarious to sustain itself for very long, and in the third paragraph it begins to dissolve: "While we loiter here this autumn evening, looking for a spot retired enough, where we shall quietly rest to-night, they thus, in that chilly March evening, one hundred and forty-two years before us, with wind and current favoring, have already glided out of sight, not to camp, as we shall, at night, but while two sleep one will manage the canoe, and the swift stream bear them onward to the settlements" (323). Thus Hannah parts company with Thoreau, as she and her companions take flight into a future that now lies deep in the American past. Her return to the past is confirmed by the episode's brief, final paragraph, whose first sentence executes the final shift of tenses: "According to the historian, they escaped as by a miracle all roving bands of Indians, and reached their homes in safety" (323). The sentence has been forced into the past tense by the presence of the historian in its initial phrase, and we feel that presence as an intrusion, in part because this is the first time that the historian's authority has been invoked.

Of course, the entire narrative belongs to the historian, whose account Thoreau has rewritten.[17] But by withholding the reference to his source almost to the end, he is able to take command of the historical materials from the outset and through careful narrative preparation achieve the extraordinary convergence of time and space of the second paragraph. Thoreau thus becomes his own historian of the river and, with the power of authorship that he has conferred upon himself, takes the episode of Hannah Duston's escape out of the dead past and recovers it for the living present. Hannah, who sails between the worlds of the dead and the living, is herself a figure for this activity.

Returning now to the episode's first sentence, we can see how it anticipated the dramatic convergence of Thoreau's and Hannah's moments on the river. The writer's historical remembrance of Hannah was prompted, he implies, by his and his brother's arrival at "this part of the river" at the same time of day as she and her companions arrived there a hundred and forty-two years earlier. This coincidence of time and place belongs to a convention common to the procedures of *A Week* and to those of much nineteenth-century travel literature: the prompting of historical incident by the fortuitous view.[18] We need now to consider more broadly the ways in which the "view," and particularly the view afforded by a river perspective, facilitates Thoreau's entry into the past.

two

≈≈≈
≈≈≈

FURTHER
DOWN
THE STREAM
OF TIME

T he rivers of *A Week* serve Thoreau's purposes of inscription
well, because, as he describes them, they are themselves an inscription—a line drawn by nature giving to the landscape a
sense of human form and boundary. It might be said, in fact, that
rivers are the most human and social bodies of water. A lake or pond,
like Thoreau's Walden, invites a solitary communion with nature; and
an ocean, such as the Atlantic of *Cape Cod,* beckons toward a vast,
lonely wilderness of space. But a river connects human places, as *A
Week*'s frequent images of commerce and scenes of social discourse
illustrate.[1]

As Thoreau explains in his first chapter, one of whose purposes is to
establish the book's controlling image, a river is already humanized
even in its undiscovered state: "Rivers must have been the guides which
conducted the footsteps of the first travellers." He writes, "They are
the natural highways of all nations" (12).* And in "Wednesday," Tho-

---

*Thoreau's sense of the river's civilizing aspect anticipates the work of later
thinkers, such as Patrick Geddes and Benton MacKaye, who recognized the distinctive role of river valleys and of the watershed in the evolution of cultural
history.

reau makes clear the superiority of rivers over literal highways: "Thus, far from the beaten highways and the dust and din of travel, we beheld the country privately, yet freely, and at our leisure. Other roads do some violence to Nature, and bring the traveller to stare at her, but the river steals into the scenery it traverses without intrusion, silently creating and adorning it, and is as free to come and go as the zephyr" (235).

The distinction Thoreau makes here between highway travel and river travel suggests the complex mode of perception that rivers enable. At the most basic level, the river perspective enhances observation simply because of the clear, unobstructed line of sight to the shore that it provides. The subject, removed entirely from the object of his vision and floating on an element different from that which he observes, is distinguished in his role *as* observer. The implications of this special view are suggested by Thoreau in an 1860 Journal entry, where he describes another, later boating experience: "To . . . see the earth from the *water side,* to stand outside of it on another element, and so get a pry on it in thought at least, that is no small advantage" (March 25, 1860: *J,* 13:226–27; Thoreau's emphasis).

This advantage applies, to some degree, even when the travelers are primarily engaged in rowing or otherwise navigating their craft. But it brings its greatest rewards at those times when current and wind relieve them of navigation entirely, allowing periods of sustained observation. When Thoreau and his brother are navigating the Merrimack upstream, during the first half of the voyage, such periods are frequent but intermittent. On their return voyage, when they are carried downstream by the Merrimack and assisted by favorable winds, the advantage of the leisurely river perspective obtains fully.

But while the river distinguishes the role of the observer, it also distances him from the object of his vision and in other ways also restricts and defines his possibilities. Because the view from a boat on a river is necessarily fleeting and dependent upon the speed and direction of the current as well as the wind, the careful, sustained examination of a scene, of the sort one associates with conventional sightseeing, is impossible. In the absence of a fixed point of view, the relation of subject to object becomes discontinuous and relative. This condition encourages a shift from observation to reflection, to the "metamorphosis" of objects on the shore, as in the following passage from "Friday": "Sitting with our faces now up stream, we studied the landscape by degrees, as one unrolls a map . . . , assuming new and varying positions as wind and water shifted the scene, and there was variety enough for our entertainment in the metamorphoses of the simplest objects. Viewed from this side the scenery appeared new to us" (349).

To make the landscape new is a way to take mental possession of it, and, on the page following the above passage, Thoreau announces his holdings: "What I see is mine. I am a large owner in the Merrimack intervals" (350). His sense of ownership here belongs in part to the special qualities of the river traveler's perspective. Its gradual pace and the slow but sweeping inclusiveness of its vision encourage imaginative appropriation. Our awareness of the privilege of this perspective can be heightened by remembering how utterly dispossessed of the landscape Thoreau feels on the bleak strand of *Cape Cod* (*CC*, 107, 147–49).[2]

Visual as opposed to palpable possession of the landscape is a familiar idea in Transcendentalist thought and needs no further elaboration here. What is most notable for us in the passage above is the way in which the imagery of a map unrolling in the mind confirms the inward, reflective vision of reality encouraged by the river's perspective. The point can be overemphasized, however. If, on the one hand, the condition of river travel encourages reflection, on the other its continual opening of new and unexpected scenes periodically commands renewed attention and observation. In fact, the interplay of these two modes of perception—observation and reflection—is one of *A Week*'s most important structuring principles.[3] It provides the context for the book's rich dialogue between inner and outer life and parallels its most fundamental symbolic opposition, that of the shore versus the river. To observe the shore (despoiled by time) and return its reflected images to the river (eternity) is to redeem it, to save it from time and confer it to the writer's imagination.

As we have seen, the very condition of river travel promotes a continuous change in perspective. But such change in *A Week* is not always fortuitous. Sometimes Thoreau deliberately manipulates his point of view to secure the altered visual experience he wants. For example, in "Sunday" he speaks of the difficulty of focusing attention on the water's reflecting surface: "We noticed that it required a separate intention of the eye, a more free and abstracted vision, to see the reflected trees and the sky, than to see the river bottom merely" (48). This "separate intention of the eye" is the mind's way of appropriating for its own higher (and inward) purposes the materials of observation. It is the work of perception.

If a shifting perspective is one of *A Week*'s most important visual strategies, another of equal importance is obscurity, or "indistinctness." Following Emerson's example, Thoreau often maneuvers himself in position to blur the hard outlines of the world in order to reveal the larger rays of relation. As he puts it in "Friday," "Sometimes we see objects as through a thin haze, in their eternal relations" (359). Though images of indistinctness appear throughout *A Week*, they have their greatest frequency in "Tuesday," the chapter that, significantly, is the most deeply layered with memory. As Thoreau and his brother pass a canal boat before sunrise on this day, the fog obscures their vision, which moves Thoreau to say, "A slight mist, through which objects are faintly visible, has the effect of expanding even ordinary streams, by a singular mirage, into arms of the sea or inland lakes" (191). And a page later he observes, "The most stupendous scenery ceases to be sublime when it becomes distinct, or in other words limited, and the imagination is no longer encouraged to exaggerate it" (192). The most dramatic and revelatory use of fog and cloud in "Tuesday," and in the book as a whole, is Thoreau's narration of his ascension of Saddleback Mountain, to which we shall return.

All the visual perspectives described above work to bring the sights of the shore into the life of imagination, where they prompt a much wider exploration through time and space (sometimes through a formal digression but more often through a spontaneous "association") than the literal voyage can provide. I mean to distinguish here between *A Week*'s surface and its depth—between its geographical, objective reality (the mere facts of the shore, witnessed in a transient moment of the present) and its inward, subjective vision (symbolized by the river's fluid but eternal current). To put it simply, Thoreau's basic procedure in *A Week* is to deliver the products of observation to his reflecting mind, which assimilates them into his developing "memory" of the rivers' history. The point can be emphasized by noting that reflection, as an activity of inward life, is itself entirely dependent upon memory. That is to say, reflection involves the past; it brings the materials of observation into the flow of human time, where "association" links elements of the past and present. In this manner, the "view" becomes still another way of entering the past.

The following passage from "Tuesday" illuminates the process by which the river perspective encourages the historical imagination: "Being on the river, whose banks are always high and generally conceal the few houses, the country appeared much more wild and primitive than to the traveller on the neighboring roads." Thoreau continues, "Sometimes this forenoon the country appeared in its primitive state, and as if the Indian still inhabited it; and again, as if many free new settlers occupied it" (194). In this case, the distant view of the shore has simplified the landscape and thus invited entry into its imagined past.[4]

But visual perception is not merely a servant to memory in *A Week*. It would be more accurate to say that, in this book, these two human capacities parallel one another, that they have complementary and mutually reinforcing roles. Both memory and perception take the outer world inward by appropriating for the individual human mind a distinctive view of reality. As we have seen, the relation of memory to time is selective; it plays and replays the past, conferring value upon certain moments. (In "Wednesday," Thoreau writes that words inspired by love "are incessantly repeated and modulated by the memory" [269].) Just as memory enters and focuses time, so too visual perception focuses (or deliberately obscures) and organizes space. And Thoreau's assimilation of various, differing historical "views" of the rivers' past has its corresponding activity in the ranging perspectivalism of the journeyers' literal vision.

Further, both memory and perception often enhance experience by rendering the world "indistinct." Just as Thoreau prefers the imprecise memories of farmers and haymakers to more objective sources of history because they lend themselves to his larger poetic purposes, so also he obscures the landscape through cloud, fog, and mist in order to find in it the larger lines of relation. We have seen how memory also is an agent of continuity because it bridges discrete moments of time and draws a line of relation from the past to the present. In this way, both memory and perception do the work of mediation and point toward the larger (cosmic) mediation that is the desideratum of all of Thoreau's work.

As a journey of the pen and mind, *A Week* voyages upon two rivers, absorbing their ever-changing scenes through the process of observation and reflection. The general direction of the journey is from the known to the unknown, from the familiar shoreline of the Concord River to the less familiar landscape of the Merrimack, where the experience of discovery intensifies.[5] When, in "Sunday," the brothers pass from the Concord River to the Merrimack through the canal and its locks, Thoreau observes, "Unlike the Concord, the Merrimack is not a dead but a living stream" (88). Though the Concord has more life in its waters (the digression on fishes takes place in "Saturday") and on its banks, the swifter current of the Merrimack becomes for Thoreau a serviceable symbol for heightened adventure. The "freedom of the Merrimack" (79)—its "buoyant tide" and its "'freer water'" (110)— carries its travelers into regions farther from home and distinctly "wilder." When, in "Monday," Thoreau and his brother examine "a new tree to us" (the bass), he notes, "The sight of this tree reminded us that we had reached a strange land to us" (158, 159). There are numerous other examples of discovery in this portion of the book. And there is no question that the digression on the Bhagavad Gita and other "ancient books" (147), which also occurs in "Monday," has the effect of radically expanding *A Week's* frame of reference—opening up new territories of the mind and spirit as the literal voyage reaches into its own new territories.

When, in "Thursday," the two brothers reach the turning point of their journey, the summit of Mount Agiocochook, we are prepared by the book's developing pattern of discovery to find considerable signifi-

cance in this moment. Unlike *Walden, A Week* is a journey book with a
mountaintop as its turning point, and inevitably it raises our expectations that it will fulfill the terms of this classic structure: progress toward the source, which, when reached, will provide enlightenment
and enable the return. We know from Thoreau's "Ktaadn, and the
Maine Woods" that he could find the mountain-climbing experience
climactic and revelatory. ("What," he asks on Mount Katahdin, "is this
Titan that has possession of me?" [*MW,* 71].) As we shall see, however, his treatment of the mountaintop experience here fails these expectations, and to understand why we need to set the context of
"Thursday," the chapter in which it occurs.

On the voyage of 1839, Thoreau and his brother concluded the river
portion of their trip on Wednesday night, September 4, and on Thursday morning began a week-long land journey that took them to the
White Mountains. After four days of hiking in the mountains they returned to their boat on the Merrimack on the following Thursday
morning, September 12, and arrived home in Concord on Friday
night. Thoreau's rendering is true to this chronology, except that he
simply reports rather than describes most of the extended land journey and thereby effectively collapses two weeks into one. The two
chronological Thursdays of the journey are contained by the chapter,
"Thursday," a purely literary space. As he was to do later in *Walden,*
Thoreau shortens his chronology by half to gain a more unified effect.

Though the formal advantages this condensation of the journey
gives to *A Week* are obvious (it makes this unequivocally a book about
voyaging), it is nevertheless puzzling that Thoreau, having chosen to
include his mountaintop experience at all, placed it in so merely inter-
stitial a position in the text. Still more puzzling is *A Week*'s flat and
perfunctory rendering of that experience. Following a brief and rou-
tine description of the climb, the phrase announcing the climbers' ascension is curiously passive—"we were enabled to reach the summit"—and is followed not by a description of that summit but instead
by verses from George Herbert's "Virtue," in an almost palpable displacement of the authorial eye. We never see the summit or its view,
and are "returned to Hooksett, a week afterward" (314) with extraordinary abruptness. Quite simply, Thoreau gives the moment away.

Why he should have done this can be explained, I believe, by remembering that long before the chapter "Thursday," *A Week* had already conveyed its climactic mountaintop experience. It had done so in "Tuesday," where the writer recalls from another expedition his ascension of Saddleback Mountain (now called Greylock). Thoreau does not mention the fact that this other expedition took place after the voyage (in 1844), and his introduction of the story ("I once saw the day break from the top of Saddle-back Mountain" [180]) suggests a memory called up from deep in the past. The context of Saddleback's appearance—the narrator-journeyer interrupting his voyage to tell a story—also leads the reader to understand it as a prior experience.

Following an extended description of his trip and of his laborious nighttime climb through an "ocean of mist," Thoreau reveals the spectacular view in "cloudland" that his efforts have earned: "As the light in the east steadily increased, it revealed to me more clearly the new world into which I had risen in the night, the new terra-firma perchance of my future life." He continues, "All around beneath me was spread for a hundred miles on every side, as far as the eye could reach, an undulating country of clouds, answering in the varied swell of its surface to the terrestrial world it veiled. It was such a country as we might see in dreams, with all the delights of paradise" (188).

That this revelatory moment (its mountaintop setting strongly suggests the culmination of a vision quest)[6] is called up from memory rather than from the present voyage is telling. The Saddleback journey—as well as the mysterious, dreamlike excursion through "a romantic and retired valley" (203) near the Connecticut River, which also is recounted from another expedition in "Tuesday"—are journeys layered within a journey, memories within a memory. To remember other journeys within the context of narrating the primary journey is to make journeying itself archetypal and therefore the property of inward life. By conferring the mountaintop experience to memory, by layering it deep within his book's time scheme rather than highlighting the climb of September 1839, Thoreau richly complicates *A Week*'s temporal dimension.[7]

Saddleback's placement at the midpoint of the book's development is appropriate and strategic; in its inwardness and its domination by two extended memories, "Tuesday" interrupts and temporarily arrests *A Week*'s developing motion of discovery. Following "Monday," with its expansive, outward-setting mood, this chapter draws us back, reminds us that *A Week,* while a travel book, is more importantly an excursion into time, and that it is licensed to travel to times and places in the writer's memory other than those of the present voyage.* It also argues implicitly that memory does not order the past sequentially but layers it into levels of value and meaning whose relation to one another is more poetic than historical. And as we saw earlier, "Tuesday"'s pervasive environment of mist, cloud, and fog is the visual equivalent for the haze of memory through which the past is viewed. The sense of "Tuesday" as a hiatus in the voyage is reinforced by the brothers' arrival in midday on "a large island" where they "lingered long" (222, 231). In every significant way, "Tuesday" is an island experience; it is the chapter in which inward life is accredited and won.†

That the primary mountaintop experience of this book is filtered through the haze of time and memory emphasizes the great difference between *A Week* and "Ktaadn." "Ktaadn" dramatized for Thoreau a confrontation with the absolute otherness of nature,[8] a confrontation that is almost purely spatial in character. In fact, the famous disorientation that the writer experienced on Mount Katahdin—"*Who* are we? *where* are we?" (*MW,* 71)—can be seen, in part, as a radical dislocation from the flow of time. *A Week,* in contrast, enacts a process that necessarily unfolds itself *in* time.[9] Rather than an abrupt encounter with the unknown, here we have a gradual attempt to bring as much as possible within the purview of the known. As we have seen, the geography of rivers encourages this gentler mode of discovery.

Upon the passage home, Thoreau states his accomplishment mod-

---

*"Monday" also contains the narration of a remembered expedition, a trip up the Nashua River valley (162–63, 165–66), but its treatment is brief and truncated. In no sense does it dominate "Monday" in the way that Saddleback and the Connecticut River valley trip dominate "Tuesday."

†By dramatizing the power of memory, "Tuesday" prepares for the more overt (rhetorical) treatment of the theme in "Wednesday," especially in that chapter's digression on friendship (259–89).

estly: "The places where we had stopped or spent the night in our way up the river, had already acquired a slight historical interest for us" (353). A few pages earlier he had cited the liabilities of a narrow geographical perspective: "It is an important epoch when a man who has always lived on the east side of a mountain, and seen it in the west, travels round and sees it in the east." The knowledge that such expanded perspective gives him is that "nature is one and continuous every where" (349). This suggests one of *A Week*'s most important connections to *Walden,* for despite their different procedures (voyaging versus inhabiting), both are records of a profound attempt to discover higher truths through an exploration of the familiar.[10] It might be more accurate to say that *A Week* anticipates *Walden* by enacting the process of discovery and assimilation (traveling around the mountain) that transforms the unknown into the familiar. Analogously, it could be said that *A Week*'s deliberate immersion in the flow of human time (history) anticipates *Walden*'s encounter with eternity.

In "Friday" Thoreau observes, "When my thoughts are sensible of change, I love to see and sit on rocks which I *have* known, and pry into their moss, and see unchangeableness so established. I not yet gray on rocks forever gray, I no longer green under the evergreens. There is something even in the lapse of time by which time recovers itself" (351; Thoreau's emphasis). The value of the known is here even more firmly established; to know the rocks is to possess a standard of permanence by which change (including the change that drives human mortality—both Thoreau's and, by implication, his brother's) may be measured and understood. Though the river images "the lapse of time," with all the tragic implications of loss that this phrase implies, the act of voyaging upon the river has "recovered" for Thoreau a sense of the eternal.

By displacing his literal mountaintop setting, then, Thoreau deepens his commitment to memory. Just as important, however, is the fact that this displacement also robs that setting of its significance as a turning point. The effect of this is to take the journey's turn out of a spatial context altogether and to give priority instead to another kind of turn—the turn of the seasons. In the opening paragraph of "Friday," the voyage's final day, Thoreau and his brother lie "awake long before day-break [at their campsite on the upper Merrimack], listening to the rippling of the river and the rustling of the leaves" for signs of "a change in the weather." Moments later, Thoreau decides: "That night was the turning point of the season. We had gone to bed in summer, and we awoke in autumn; for summer passes into the autumn in some unimaginable point of time, like the turning of a leaf" (334).

We can now see the further significance of Thoreau's having collapsed the time of his journey by a week. By deferring the book's true turning point from "Thursday," the chapter that narrates the ascension of Agiocochook and the beginning of the return voyage down the Merrimack, to the beginning of "Friday," he permits the historical time with which the voyage began to overtake and synchronize itself with the naturally measured time of nature. The arbitrary measurement of time called a week has been replaced by nature's own time in the great moment of the season's turn.[11]

Thoreau tried through the life of his Journal to locate the "unimaginable point of time" of the season's turn that he marks with such certainty in the passage above. The Journal, in its very nature, is a record of discrete observations and tentative conclusions about nature's larger rhythms and their possible significance for the individual human mind. But the narrative context of *A Week* permits Thoreau to bring natural and human time into full "correspondence," thus realizing in a moment what the larger document realizes only provisionally and incrementally over a period of more than two decades. In part, the book's elegiac intention allows this by encouraging resolution. But more important is its synthetic form*—the form of a "week." So short

*The individual chapters are also syntheses. Many of their elements, such as literary analogue and historical anecdote, are insertions of journal and essay material that interrupt the narrative. Yet the interruptions make vivid the presence of the authorial self, testing an experience of 1839 against the fund of reading and thinking invested since the voyage. Less important to Thoreau than narrative development is his complex exploration of the self in time. *A Week*'s discursiveness, seen by James Russell Lowell and many subsequent critics as a liability, may thus be considered an expression of its basic procedures. These procedures are examined most comprehensively in Johnson, *Thoreau's Complex Weave;* see also Buell, *Literary Transcendentalism,* chap. 8.

and arbitrary a unit of time, a week becomes the opening into the mystery of time itself. Its very arbitrariness is a mark of the human desire to penetrate that mystery, and its brevity places it in a microcosmic relation to time, in something of the same way that the "little world" (130) of *Walden* symbolizes the cosmos.

Following the brothers' awakening into autumn at the beginning of "Friday," they set their boat in the water and begin "to sweep downward with the rushing river" (335). At almost every stage of the return voyage down the Merrimack, the brothers are assisted by the elements, as they "sailed fleetly before the wind" (348) and make their "rapid downward passage" (353). From the reader's point of view, this speeding of the travelers' pace adds to the sense of disproportion between the two parts of the journey. The effect of collapsing two Thursdays into one had been to give five and a half "days" to the voyage away from Concord and only one and a half to the return. Now, by accelerating that already abbreviated return, Thoreau creates the sense of a "rush" homeward.

The disproportion between the two parts of the voyage can be understood symbolically in the following way. Having encountered and challenged time in its "concrete," historical character on the voyage away from Concord, the travelers have earned free passage home on the river of time (timelessness, "myth") in whose eternal current they are now privileged to "float" for a while. Even though given frequently to moments of reflection, the voyage away from Concord can, in retrospect, be seen as essentially "outward bound," in the full psychic meaning of this phrase: bound, committed, to the outward world— the world of the shore—whose facts and history it is charged to absorb. The return voyage, correspondingly, is "inward bound," which is to say, bound toward the deepest center of the self, into the current of being (*Walden*'s "circulations") for which the river is both symbol and vehicle. That is, attention shifts from the shore, which exists in and has been despoiled by time, to the river, Thoreau's symbol for eternity: "we observed less what was passing on the shore, than the dateless associations and impressions which the season awakened, anticipating in some measure the progress of the year" (348–49).

When the brothers pass through the locks on "Friday," they are glad to see again the locksman with whom they had shared a poignant moment on the voyage out (79), but on this occasion they "did not stop to consider any of his problems" (361). The passage through the canal is given only a sentence this time, and upon their arrival at the Concord River the weather turns warm: "This change in the weather was favorable to our contemplative mood, and disposed us to dream yet deeper at our oars, while we floated in imagination further down the stream of time." "Chelmsford and Billerica," Thoreau continues, "appeared like old English towns, compared with Merrimack and Nashua, and many generations of civil poets might have lived and sung here" (366). The dream and contemplation of this passage signal the full shift from *A Week*'s surface to its depth. At this point in the book, the brothers have traveled as far "down" toward the center of consciousness as their voyage can take them. And their journeying into unknown regions has rewarded them by fully historicizing their native ground; they have made history.

This shift accounts for the extraordinary quality of convergence that the final chapter achieves. Here observation and reflection meet in "contemplation," and, as we have seen, human and natural time come together. Terms that were earlier set in stark opposition, such as history-myth and science-poetry, begin to show signs of reconciliation. Most importantly, fact joins symbol, as Thoreau comes to understand that he has "need to be earth-born as well as heaven-born" (380). "Is not Nature, rightly read," he asks, "that of which she is commonly taken to be the symbol merely?" (382). "Friday" communicates an intense love of the earth: "Here or nowhere is our heaven" (380). And fittingly, Thoreau's profound sense of being at home in the world is best expressed here by his image of "rivers flowing through valleys" (380).

Summer, the setting of the outward voyage, had been a time of joy and adventure, but autumn is for contemplation: "In summer, we live out of doors, and have only impulses and feelings, which are all for action, and must wait commonly for the stillness and longer nights of autumn and winter before any thought will subside" (377). Autumn brings "the true harvest of the year" (378), a harvest of thought, and has its corresponding image in the sunset that Thoreau and his brother witness as they approach Concord: "Though the shadows of the hills were beginning to steal over the stream, the whole river valley undulated with mild light, purer and more memorable than the noon" (389). Not only is the sunset memorable, it also stands for memory; its attendant twilight "holds" the day, gathers it in as the autumn gathers in the year. The twin powers of memory and perception have, in *A Week,* filtered the historical and visual life of two rivers and made of them one river of the imagination. Thoreau brings all of it home (literally) to Concord, which is the beginning and the end of the voyage, and the symbolic center of the self for him.

Upon the brothers' departure from Concord in "Saturday," their orientation had been lovingly retrospective, with "our faces turned [backward] towards" a Concord fisherman, "the last of our townsmen whom we saw" (23). Now, on "Friday," their orientation is eagerly prospective as they race home: "Thus we sailed, not being able to fly, but as next best, making a long furrow in the fields of the Merrimack toward our home, with our wings spread" (360). As they sail into their "native port" that evening, they find "still preserved" in the flattened grass of "the Concord mud" the outline of their keel, and this is not the only evidence that remains of their earlier presence. After having "leaped gladly on shore," they secure their boat "to the wild apple-tree, whose stem still bore the mark which its chain had worn in the chafing of the spring freshets" (393). Unlike the disregarded nail in the apple tree of Tyngsborough, this mark confirms remembrance and continuity. As the book's closing image, it completes the work of inscription that is the achievement of *A Week.*

The writing of *A Week* helped Thoreau to understand that, paradoxically, an immersion in the flow of time was necessary to overcome time, and that he would have to confront and experience the destructive force of history in order to recover from it his own and his region's lost past. The problem of *A Week,* however, as a comprehensive response to the issue of time that his brother's death had focused for him was that even though it was, as he called it, an "unroofed book" (*PJ*, 3 : 279)—one day's voyaging adventure opening provisionally on the next—it was essentially an elegiac and retrospective response to experience. The fragments recovered and synthesized belonged largely to the past. Built upon a journey with a beginning and an end, its linear form called for—and received, in its lyrical closing chapter—resolution and closure. In view of the longer-term requisites of Thoreau's life and career, this was both the achievement and the limitation of *A Week*.

For all its rivering upon the stream of time, *A Week* could not open itself to the living instant of the present, the nick of time. While it bore lessons for the conduct of life, it could not provide an overarching context in which the future could be confidently anticipated. Thoreau needed a book that could commemorate the past as faithfully as *A Week* had, but also in the very act of composition replicate the continuous issuance (or what Whitman called "efflux") of time into the world, and, through the comprehensiveness of its perspective, draw the design of the future. Such a book would be even more unroofed than *A Week:* it would have no beginning and no end.

PART 2
THE JOURNAL

Knowledge of sensible realities thus comes to life inside the tissue of experience. It is *made;* and made by relations that unroll themselves in time. . . . According to my view, experience as a whole is a process in time, whereby innumerable particular terms lapse and are superseded by others that follow upon them by transitions which, whether disjunctive or conjunctive in content, are themselves experiences, and must in general be accounted at least as real as the terms which they relate.

—William James, "A World of Pure Experience"

≋≋≋

three

PICTURING
THE WORLD

horeau's Journal is a lifework, in the sense that it ultimately became his central literary concern, but also in the literal sense
that it belonged to his life. It is as much a part of that life as the
writer's daily walks, to which it is closely related.[1] When the life begins
to fail under the debilitating effects of tuberculosis, the Journal becomes intermittent and finally falls silent, but it never really ends. In
fact, if the reports of Thoreau's serene acceptance of death in his final
days are true, his life ended with a far greater sense of closure than
does the Journal. Its final entry, like all the thousands that precede it,
stands there expectant, awaiting another.[2]

If we are unable to locate an entry that marks the Journal's formal
close, we have no trouble finding the one that marks its inauguration.
It was written on October 22, 1837, shortly after Thoreau's graduation
from Harvard, and begins: " 'What are you doing now?' he asked, 'Do
you keep a journal?'— So I make my first entry to-day" (*PJ*, 1:5). The
unnamed "he" is almost certainly Emerson, and the pedagogical force
of the question is unmistakable. By 1837, Emerson had been keeping
his own journal for seventeen years and, convinced of its inestimable

value to his own growth, had encouraged others in his circle to do so. This private discipline of mind and spirit had a significant public and collective aspect as well, for it was the practice of these Emersonians to share their journal writing with one another and even sometimes to publish excerpts in the *Dial*. So much a part of the regimen of the Transcendentalists' way of life did journal keeping eventually become that at least one of Emerson's followers forced the discipline on his unwilling children.[3]

Thoreau did not need to be forced; he responded to Emerson's call with the fervor of a disciple, eagerly taking up the literary instrument that, the Transcendentalists believed, was best suited for capturing the inspiration of one's genius in the moment of its inception. The point, of course, is that in initiating a journal, he was joining a going concern, jumping aboard the express train of radical thought in America in the 1830s, and adopting one of its requisite practices. This is the sense in which Thoreau's Journal may be said to have no beginning. The telling connective "so" ("So I make my first entry to-day") suggests not only the student's obedience to his teacher's call but also the almost automatic, gestural quality of his action.

Given this context, Thoreau's Journal in its first weeks and months is exactly what we would anticipate: a highly self-conscious and studentlike practice board of ideas. Initially, these ideas are grouped according to topics designated by headings, such as "Solitude," "Beauty," "Truth," and "Harmony." By 1840, the headings have dropped away and the entries have become more flowing, interrelated, and organic—their evolving form reflecting the originality and sophistication that increase steadily through the new decade.* The volume called Long Book, which Thoreau kept from the fall of 1842 to March 1846 (roughly, from the time of his brother's death to the period of the Walden experiment), as well as the several volumes he kept at the Pond between 1845 and 1847, richly anticipate both *A Week* and *Walden*. Numerous

---

*What we have of Thoreau's earliest Journal volumes—those he kept from 1837 through mid-1842—are versions the author transcribed from their (largely) missing originals. See Robert Sattelmeyer, "Historical Introduction," *PJ,* 1:596–606.

passages from these works appear well formed in their earlier journal versions.

But for all the increasing sophistication of its entries, the Journal of the 1840s, considered as a whole, lacks the sense of a coherent literary undertaking—that is, the sense of an integral, self-contained set of purposes transcending the document's use as a source book and workshop for ideas. One obvious indication of this is its physically fragmentary nature: Thoreau cannibalized his Journal in this period for his other writings, freely pulling extracts from it for use in lectures and essays and in drafts of *A Week* and *Walden*.

However, as modern scholarship has discovered, he altered this practice in 1850 and began to preserve his Journal entries in full, usually by copying out the material he wished to employ elsewhere.[4] This discovery has large implications, the most important of which is its confirmation of what Perry Miller recognized many years ago as a significant departure. Miller noticed that in the early 1850s the Journal becomes "a deliberately constructed work of art."[5] There is no doubt that the entries written in this period have a far more consistently formal, elegant, and coherent aspect than those that appear earlier. By 1851, Thoreau is writing not only in his Journal but for it as well.

Miller had a ready explanation for this striking development. It owed, he said, to the writer's disappointment at the commercial and critical failure of *A Week on the Concord and Merrimack Rivers*. Because of this public failure, Miller argued, Thoreau turned his attention to the making of a private book, his Journal. Its success would always be measured by his own standards rather than those of the literary marketplace. As ballast for this theory of compensation, Miller cited a Journal passage of January 27, 1852, in which Thoreau speculates that "thoughts written down thus in a journal might be printed in the same form with greater advantage—than if the related ones were brought together into separate essays" (*J*, 3:239). Miller found here evidence that Thoreau "was crying 'sour grapes' about something he desperately wanted [public acclaim as the author of books and essays] but could not get. . . . [T]he tone to notice is the alacrity with which he was accommodating himself to defeat."[6]

This severe judgment, proceeding from Miller's characteristic animus toward Thoreau, has been surprisingly influential,[7] but it needs revision. That Thoreau was disappointed in the public failure of his first book is certain. But to say that this disappointment alone accounts for the maturation of his Journal is to ignore the imperatives of form and development within the work itself. The most misleading aspect of Miller's formulation is the exclusive emphasis on the Journal's emergence as "a work of art." By considering this document's developing coherence solely in terms of the writer's formal objectives, Miller misinterprets the way in which Thoreau understood the evolution of art out of thought and experience. Form, for Thoreau, is not an end in itself, but rather the result of an organic process of discovery—of self and world. This is not to deny that Thoreau wanted to be a writer, which he clearly, and sometimes desperately, did. But he conceived of this vocation, as Sherman Paul has demonstrated, as a full spiritual calling that required something more than attention to craft as such.[8] Before Thoreau could begin to entertain the formal possibilities of his Journal, it was necessary first to reconsider its most fundamental human purpose.

KEEPING TIME: THE ART OF MEMORY

In an entry made in January or early February 1851, a year before the passage cited by Miller, Thoreau declares: "I would fain keep a journal which should contain those thoughts & impressions which I am most liable to forget that I have had   Which would have, in one sense the greatest remoteness—in another the greatest nearness, to me" (*PJ,* 3 : 178). The closing phrases of this passage rehearse the writer's familiar penchant for abstracting experience into its most essential aspect. But its initial portion states a specifically commemorative purpose for the Journal and asserts this as a new imperative. For Thoreau to have suddenly asked himself for such a journal—a repository of valued thought and experience, a kind of surrogate memory—fourteen years after he had begun to keep a journal seems an unlikely development, since this document had always implicitly served him in this way. Yet what is happening here is a rediscovery, a deepening of awareness, a coming into fuller knowledge of what is already known, with a fresh understanding of the implications of prior practice.

The preservation of experience endangered by loss was, of course, a central theme of *A Week,* and it seems to me likely that Thoreau's sharpened sense of his Journal's commemorative purpose—reflected in many of the entries during this period[9]—is a direct outgrowth of what he had learned in thinking through the development of that work. This purpose, rather than disappointment in commercial failure, is the most important legacy of *A Week* to the mature Journal, and establishes an authentically generative relation between what may be considered Thoreau's first and second "books." It may also be true that the formal elegance of the writer's post-1850 Journal owes, in part, to the way in which the composition of *A Week* taught him how the "day" might be used creatively as a synthetic unit of thought. Furthermore, the Journal's increased formality and coherence in this period can be attributed to the care that Thoreau was now giving to the act of commemoration.

In the years after the publication of *Walden* (1854), Thoreau's insight that his Journal could preserve for him what otherwise would be lost to the attritions of time and experience is fully consolidated, as a passage from February 5, 1855, suggests: "In a journal it is important in a few words to describe the weather, or character of the day, as it affects our feelings. That which was so important at the time cannot be unimportant to remember" (*J,* 7:171). But, as I have indicated, Thoreau was already moving toward this insight in the earliest days of 1851, and the entries of the subsequent weeks and months reveal a steadily deepening understanding of the Journal's commemorative purpose. Although the following passage from an August 19, 1851, entry does not specifically refer to the Journal, it nevertheless displays an important new emphasis: "What if a man were earnestly & wisely to set about recollecting & preserving the thoughts which he has had! How many perchance are now irrecoverable!— Calling in his neighbors to aid him" (*PJ,* 3:379).

What Thoreau is implicitly describing here is a book of memory;

and a passage written in the following year reveals the Journal's newly enlarged purpose: "A Journal.—a book that shall *contain* a record of *all* your joy—your extacy" (July 13, 1852: *J*, 4:223; emphases added). I mean to stress here the Journal's special capacity for comprehensiveness. Other kinds of books (such as *A Week*) tell only the "story" of a life, which is to say, a retrospective and necessarily selective rendering. But a journal renders the life as lived, comprehensively; it "contain[s] a record" not only of "all your joy" but also of apparently incidental experiences or perceptions whose hidden significance might later emerge as part of a larger pattern or, conversely, as an important departure from the normal round. One can never know precisely what is important to remember in the moment; only time will tell.

To read one's journal is both to reexperience the discrete moments of time past—thus commemorating them—and to tally those moments against the present as a way of measuring change. A passage from a September 12, 1851, entry shows Thoreau reading his Journal specifically for the purpose of comparing past and present. The results surprise him: "I can hardly believe that there is so great a diffirence between one year & another as my journal shows. The 11th of this month last year the river was as high as it commonly is in the spring— over the causeway on the Corner Road. It is now quite low. Last year Oct 9th the huckleberries were fresh & abundant on Conantum— They are now already dried up" (*J*, 2:498). Though the particular change—the level of the river—revealed by the Journal in this case does not in itself have great importance, the incremental force of hundreds of such observations is to show Thoreau the very nature of change—its largest rhythms and patterns. Most important, such knowledge of change reveals what in nature is unchanging, and the climactic moment in *Walden,* when Thoreau recognizes the Pond's utter permanence ("all the change is in me" [193]), owes its authenticity precisely to the double vision of experience that the Journal affords. That moment is earned by the Journal.

The daily procedure of the Journal, as it developed in the early 1850s, suggests this double vision. As Robert Sattelmeyer has said,

Thoreau "set aside regular intervals, usually in the morning, for [the Journal's] composition, and typically wrote several days' entries at a sitting, working from notes that he accumulated during his [afternoon] walks" of the previous several days.[10] Thus journal-writing became (literally) Thoreau's "morning work," that most efficacious of human activities celebrated in the first chapter of *Walden*. Morning work awakened Thoreau, made him systematically alert to what the next day's observations might reveal. But it also drew his attention to the "prior"—the perceptions of yesterday and the day before, which, when brought forward into the act of composition, established their relation to the present. More than any other of his works, the Journal provided Thoreau with the literary context for "toe[ing] that line" between "past and future" (*Wa*, 17).

Later in the 1850s, Thoreau's comparisons of natural phenomena from different seasons and years would become far more systematic and extensive than they had been early in the decade, though even in this period he was preparing for this development, making indexes to his Journal volumes. It is clear that by the fall of 1851 the Journal is already what might be called a material memory, a book deliberately conceived to "keep" time by enlarging the temporal view of reality through the process of cross-reference.[11] Increasingly, this process becomes Thoreau's major strategy for translating facts into truths—the imperative first publicly expressed in his early essay, "Natural History of Massachusetts" (1842).[12] Facts would, that is, gain spiritual significance through their gradually revealed placement along the span of time. The disciplined recording of alert observation would provide an invaluable record of facts that, when later remembered (or, reconfigured) in relation to other facts, might reveal the direction and nature of change. When the past was viewed in this way—and *viewing* is indeed the right word—it might become possible to "see" time, and to see it whole, as a full matrix of past, present, and even future.

In other words, at the same time in the early 1850s that Thoreau is discovering he can keep time through the power of commemoration, he is also discovering that he can keep time in still another, closely related sense: by spatializing the temporal process. At a key moment in the spring of 1852, this conception breaks through into overt awareness. The momentousness of the breakthrough is signaled by the initial phrase of the following Journal passage: "For the first time I perceive this spring that the year is a circle— I see distinctly the spring arc thus far. It is drawn with a firm line" (April 18, 1852: *J,* 3:438).

Like Thoreau's insight regarding his Journal's potential for commemorating experience, this discovery must be understood as a deepening of an already perceived truth. By 1852, he had for many years been an acute and faithful observer of seasonal change and had already written several drafts of *Walden,* a book that from the outset was structured according to the seasons. That he should at this late date have reacted profoundly to his perception of an age-old truth, the cyclical nature of seasonal change, may be difficult to comprehend.[13]

Yet this, I believe, was an entirely authentic discovery for Thoreau—indeed, the most important and determinative in his imaginative life. To understand its full importance, we need to place strong emphasis on his use of the word *see* in the entry's second sentence: "I *see* distinctly the spring arc thus far." What Thoreau announces here is that he has, for the first time, apprehended the temporal flow of nature's change in clearly spatial terms; he has set temporality on a plane, an "arc," along whose rim rides the flow of time. In this way, time is "contained" and given a boundary, one that coincides with consciousness itself. The "line" that describes the circle, "drawn" by the divine artist from whom all time flows, is "firm." Unlike the porous, multiple figures of Emerson's essay "Circles" (1841), expanding ever outward "wheel without wheel" (*CW,* 2:180), Thoreau's circle is unitary. Like Walden Pond, it characteristically looks inward from its perimeter toward its own deep and complex interior. Emerson's "breakthrough into spaciousness," described by David Porter, has a distinctly different character from Thoreau's equally dramatic breakthrough.[14]

From the moment Thoreau apprehends the circle of time, he remains steadily faithful to its implications. The intensity of his commitment to this design may remind us of William Butler Yeats's commitment to the "great wheel" in *A Vision* (1937),[15] which, like Thoreau's own wheel of the turning seasons, answered the poet's deepest need for an ordering structure of reality. The key point is that Thoreau's wheel is visible, of notice itself—an image of processual change that, phenological variations notwithstanding, is orderly, "regular," and dependable.

The impact of Thoreau's discovery in 1852 is everywhere evident in his later writings. Most obviously, it informs *Walden,* whose purity of spatial vision and sense of timelessness contrast markedly with *A Week*'s deliberate engagement with time. But it has its most profound effect on the Journal, where Thoreau's daily observations reveal an increasingly sure sense of nature's spatial and temporal coherence. The ease with which he begins to travel imaginatively around the circle of time is suggested by an entry of March 4, 1854. Here the fragrance of a plant "carries me back or forward to an incredible season" (*J,* 6:149). Analogously, the Journal of the early 1850s exhibits more and more frequently a syntactical conflation of past and future, such as Thoreau's reference to "days which remind me of the Indian summer that is to come" (September 21, 1854: *J,* 7:47). In many entries during this period, we find the writer virtually identifying phenomena of past and future, as in phrases such as "that reminiscence or prophesying of spring" (February 11, 1853: *J,* 4:492). When time is conceptualized as a circle, memory and anticipation come together as a single timeless dimension of experience.

Thoreau's articulation of his spatial vision of reality culminates in a set of charts, sometimes known as the "Kalendar," which he developed and drew up near the end of his life, between 1860 and 1862. These charts, several of which depict single months of the year, are an attempt to lay out all of nature's phenomena on a flat plane, that is, to graph their temporality and make a comprehensive picture of time. Each monthly chart lists down its left margin a long and varied set of natural phenomena (such as the occurrence of frost or the level of the river); across the top of the page we find the headings 1852, 1853, and so on through 1860 or, in one case, 1861. The lines Thoreau drew to coordinate the vertical (phenomenal) and horizontal (chronological) dimensions form a grid, the spaces of which he filled in with his particular observations from the Journal of these years—working from

lists he had made earlier by culling the Journal.* The act of transferring these observations from his Journal, where they are necessarily
embedded in a temporal context, in the very flux of time, to the charts,
where they stand utterly flat on the page as derived spatial abstrac-
tions, replicates the essential impulse of the mature Journal. Whatever
specific intentions Thoreau had for these documents, and however one
may judge their philosophical or scientific efficacy, they must be seen
as the ultimate extension of the Journal itself—a reflection of its inherent purpose since at least 1852.[16]

Frances Yates, in *The Art of Memory,* describes the way in which
orators of antiquity converted the materials of memory into spatial (architectural) form. This process, of course, was merely an exercise en-
abling them to master vast amounts of information.[17] But, as Yates
shows, a deepening of the relation of memory to spatial imagery occurred in the medieval art of Ramon Lull and other thinkers of the
Middle Ages, where "memory serves to visualize a cosmological and
philosophical system, a spatial pattern, whose relational aspects are ex-
plored by the searching mind." These words summarizing Yates's argument belong to Rudolf Arnheim, who broadens her discussion from
its context in medieval cosmology to a fundamental human need.
"Man is given," he says, "the task of coping with mortality—not only
his own but also that of all other constituents of his world," and to this
task he brings the art of memory, which is nothing less than a "transla-
tion of time into space," a way of overcoming "the mortality of the
present moment."[18]
Thoreau grasped in the early 1850s that his Journal might embody
for him the art of memory in the sense that it could faithfully record
and preserve his most valued perceptions, *and* that it might help him
organize these perceptions into a unified vision of life:

*These previously unpublished documents are in the Pierpont Morgan Library,
New York City. A portion of the chart for November (the month that runs to 1861)
is illustrated in the Appendix. Thoreau's Kalendar is apparently incomplete; the
Morgan file (MA 610) contains monthly charts only for April, May, June, and November. However, it contains several other documents of similar appearance, size,
and format, including one that focuses on the leafing of various trees and another
that charts the phenomena of the winter season.

It is surprising how any reminiscence of a different season of the year affects us— When I meet with any such in my journal it affects me as poetry and I appreciate that other season and that particular phenomenon more than at the time.— The world so seen is all one spring & full of beauty.— You only need to make a faithful record of an average summer day's experience & summer mood—& read it in the winter—& it will carry you back to more than that summer day alone could show—only the rarest flavor—the purest melody—of the season thus comes down to us. [*J*, 5:454]

This Journal entry was written on October 26, 1853, less than a year before the publication of *Walden,* and it anticipates *Walden's* distillation of remembered experience. But the passage itself is also such a distillation. It begins with Thoreau's delighted surprise at what his Journal can do for him, though quickly affirming his absolute confidence in it ("You only need to make a faithful record"). Reflecting upon its capacity to preserve a newborn summer's day, he implicitly shows how the Journal—always positioned at the forward edge of experience—captures what in *Walden* he called "the bloom of the present moment" (111). But his purpose here is to explain how that moment, now recaptured as he rereads the Journal, becomes "poetry" through the act of commemoration, through the mediating, enhancing effects of memory itself—thus suggesting that for him art is intimately related to memory, in some sense *is* memory.[19] The vision attained through this process is one of pure spatial coherence ("The world so seen is all one spring")—another anticipation of *Walden.* In all these ways, this Journal entry of 1853 shows us how Thoreau discovered, within a book he was already writing, his book of memory.

THE RELATIONAL IMAGINATION:
TOWARD AN AESTHETIC OF NATURE

It is no accident that Thoreau's apprehension of the circle of time is contemporaneous with his initial reading of the works of William Gilpin, the English aesthetician of nature. Though Thoreau himself does not, in his writings, link these two developments, both of them confirm the full emergence of his visual imagination. In the 1850s, Thoreau gave himself much more systematically than he ever had before to an examination of landscape views—testing his own perceptions against those of Gilpin and, later, those of John Ruskin.[20]

That Thoreau is preeminently a visual writer has been obscured by comparisons with Emerson's famous ocularity. It is true that Thoreau's relation to nature is more broadly sentient, more aural and tactile, than Emerson's, but his spiritual vocation is, if anything, even more dependent on vision (that is, on real seeing) than that of his mentor. None of his writings show this more clearly than his mature Journal, which presents a complex picture of the natural world.[21]

Glimpses of the Journal's picture can be obtained from even a brief inspection of this document, the overwhelming majority of whose seven thousand pages (in the 1906 edition) contain landscape description. Such a brief inspection cannot, however, tell us what the picture, in its vast, composite nature, looks like. For the *speculum mundi*— "the look of the world"—presented by the Journal, we need first to consider the purpose of its aesthetic vision.

On one level, this purpose is easy to define: it is to dramatize the central Emersonian belief that "Nature is the symbol of spirit" (*CW,* 1:25). This was true, for Emerson, not only in a general sense but in a very particular sense as well. "Every natural fact," he wrote in *Nature,* "is a symbol of some spiritual fact" (*CW,* 1:18). Taking this directive more seriously and literally than any other of the Concord Transcendentalists, Thoreau made himself deeply attentive to natural objects whose structure and design suggested symbolic meaning: the turtle's shell ("What mean these turtles, these coins of the muddy mint issued in early spring?" [February 23, 1857: *J,* 9:278]); the snow-laden pines, with their "*glyphic*" import (January 12, 1860: *J,* 13:86); the "rill of melted snow" in which the "laws . . . by which the world was made . . . are seen in full operation" (March 16, 1858: *J,* 10:299); or the lily, which for him was "the emblem of purity" (August 5, 1858: *J,* 11:70).[22]

Thoreau was alert to the perception of such objects and scenes, which prompted the symbolic imagination toward decipherment of nature's encoded meanings.[23] The perceiver's understanding of the meaning of these objects, whether hieroglyphic (the snow-laden pines), emblematic (the lily), or merely suggestive of nature's higher laws (the melted rill of snow), requires a naturalist's care for close observation, as well as a penchant for hermeneutics. They are to be "read," studied like a text, and the observer's posture toward them is characteristically "downward," into the mysteries of interpretation.

But nature's symbols can be found by directing the eyes upward as well, especially toward scenes of atmospheric illumination: the brilliant sunset, sunlight glinting through mist, or illumined clouds of fine reticulation, such as the "hieroglyphics in the winter sky" (*J*, 13:109) that Thoreau described in January 1860. The Journal contains many such scenes. Light as a symbol of spirit is an image as old as Western thought, but in mid-nineteenth-century America it had special importance as a symbol of both cultural promise and personal enlightenment. We find it, on the one hand, in the dramatic (often allegorical) skies of Thomas Cole and, on the other, in the more subtle spirituality of paintings in the luminist school, which has been convincingly linked to the thought of both Emerson and Thoreau.[24] For both of these thinkers, atmospheric illumination suggested the possibility of a direct, unmediated relation to the Transcendent. Perhaps the Journal's most vivid example of such an image is the rainbow, the observation of which gave rise to the following passage Thoreau wrote on August 6, 1852:

> The rainbow after all does not attract our attention proportionate to its singularity and beauty.— Moses? was the last to comment on it. It is a phenomenon more aside from the common course of nature— Too distinctly a sign—symbol of something to be disregarded. What form of beauty could be imagined more striking & conspicuous— An arch of of [sic] the most brilliant & glorious colors completely spanning heavens before the eyes of men. Children look at it. It is wonderful that all men do not take pains to behold it. At some waterfalls it is permanent as long as the sun shines. Plainly thus the maker of the Universe sets the seal to his covenant with men—many articles are thus clinched. Designed to impress man— All men beholding it be-

gin to understand the significance of the Greek epithet applied
to the world—name for the world—Kosmos or beauty. It was
designed to impress man. We live as it were within the calyx of a
flower. [*J,* 4:284–85]

The passage shows that Thoreau has moved beyond the Puritans' figural understanding of the providential "sign" to his own romantically
derived, and thus individualized, form of symbolism.[25] Yet for him, as
for his Puritan ancestors, the rainbow is laden with meaning. This passage was written only a few months after Thoreau's discovery of the
circle of time, and his intense privileging of this most resplendent of
nature's spherical forms echoes his sense of the world as an enclosure;
the rainbow is certain proof that we "live . . . within the calyx of a
flower." This, as well as other symbolic meanings that interpretation
might offer, are for Thoreau clearly embodied *in* the scene, which is
self-sufficient and self-contained. For all its evanescence and intricacy
of design, there is no mistaking the rainbow's symbolic import. It
stands forth as clearly for Thoreau as it did for Frederic Church in his
great painting "Niagara" (1857), where the rainbow is indeed a "permanent" feature of the scene it overarches.

The rainbow is more easily "read" than are scenes like the glyphic
pines, because of its dramatic presencing "above" the landscape. Moreover, its meanings have acquired greater cultural fixity, as reflected in
Thoreau's evocation of its traditional "covenant" symbolism. But the
rainbow and the pines are linked in one important respect. Both are
characterized by what may be called a vertical relation to the Transcendent. Whether looking "up" or "down," Thoreau finds in these
forms fully encoded, complete, and sufficient symbols (even if their
exact meanings are not always self-evident); they require no attendant
imagery to confirm their status or to facilitate the symbolic process.
For Thoreau and other romantic writers living in the age of Emerson,
the vertical symbol is always at its heart linguistic: an encoding of the
"word," *logos,* a complex language inscribed upon the natural world.[26]

Emerson's confidence in the human capacity to "read" nature's symbols was grounded in his belief in a "radical correspondence between

visual things and human thoughts." For him, "all spiritual facts are represented by natural symbols [which] . . . make the original elements of all languages." To see nature symbolically was to return to the "first language" and to discover in the landscape a spirituality that was "connate" with one's own inner life (*CW*, 1 : 19, 20, 10). That is, correspondence for Emerson is a process that points "upward" and "inward." Nature is the (potentially symbolic) medium through which one makes contact with Emerson's Oversoul or gains fuller knowledge of Thoreau's higher laws, and in doing so discovers the spirituality that lies within.

As an inheritor of Emersonian thought, Thoreau was inevitably compelled by the spiritual truths that nature might disclose. But one of the things that distinguishes him from Emerson is the extraordinary patience with which he was prepared to wait for their revelation. As he put it in a Journal entry of September 7, 1851: "If by watching all day & all night—I may detect some trace of the Ineffable—then will it not be worth the while to watch?" (*J*, 2 : 471). The indirect modes of apprehension to which Thoreau is most characteristically given suggest his patience: perceiving reflections or hearing echoes, tracking and tracing patterns in the grass or snow, listening for the silence that reveals spiritual presence, "seeing with the side of the eye," or hearing "with the side of the ear" (April 28 and 30, 1856: *J*, 8 : 314, 319). Like his Puritan ancestors, he was suspicious of revelation too easily earned, and, indeed, it was a principal article of faith with him that nature's truths could not be forced. In an entry of September 13, 1852, he remarks, "the more you look the less you will observe," and counsels himself: "Be not preoccupied with looking. Go not to the object let it come to you. . . . What I need is not to look at all—but a true sauntering of the eye" (*J*, 4 : 351).

But there is more than patience at work here, for something deep in Thoreau preferred to dwell on the concrete, particular forms of the natural world—those forms, with which he contrasts the rainbow, proceeding from "the common course of nature." In an entry of December 25, 1851, he writes, "Let me not be in haste to detect the *universal law*, let me see more clearly a particular instance" (*J*, 3 : 157). He

believed that if he gave close attention to such "instances" and, especially, observed relations between them, nature would slowly reveal
her secrets to him.

The effect of Thoreau's preference for dwelling in the world, rather
than leaping beyond its "instances," is essentially to flatten the vertical
design of Emerson's metaphysic, which is to say that Thoreau works
primarily in a "horizontal" framework of perception. Though he was
fascinated by vertical (singular, focused, "symbolic") images like the
rainbow, and though his Journal contains numerous passages showing
him struggling to interpret their meanings, they are not the characteristic subject of his descriptions of nature.[27] In a horizontal framework
of perception, the most characteristic object of vision is the relation
between one feature of the landscape and another. Thoreau's Journal,
as it records the landscape's diverse scenes, becomes the instrument
for a ranging cross-examination of the world. To acquire meaning, he
seems to say, every natural object must be seen in relation to another,
and then still another. Only in the incremental development of dozens,
hundreds, finally thousands, of visual relations does the writer create
the full analogical framework—the fully contextualized, composite
view—in which an authentic relation to the Ineffable may be achieved.

Another way to say this is that Emerson's thought, for all his desire
to find spirituality in the world, remains essentially neo-Platonic. He
gives just as much emphasis to "relation" as does Thoreau, but what
most concerns him is the "ray of relation [that] passes from every
other being to [the human soul]" (*CW,* 1 : 19)—the visual relation that
returns the world's diverse objects to the subject's inner life, where these
are integrated and transformed. Thoreau, on the other hand, is more
interested in the relations between the objects themselves. Though
Emerson's "correspondence" is, as Sherman Paul has shown, a "sym-
pathetic" agency—conceived to bridge the chasm between mind and
world that resulted from two centuries of Cartesianism—the metaphysical structure in which this agency does its work is essentially du-
alistic.[28] For him, spirit remains "above" rather than "within" the visual field; in the right spirit, one sees through nature to something
beyond it.

This is the force of the famous "transparent eyeball" passage in *Nature,* where the landscape becomes translucent to Emerson's visionary eye. The intense drama of perception that characterizes this passage results not from the interplay of various landscape views; rather, the speaker's vision moves immediately from "the bare common" to "the distant line of the horizon" (*CW,* 1 : 10), where all perspectives coalesce into an opalescent unity.[29] Here the perceiver finds a visual equivalent, or "symbol," for his own transformation and empowerment. Thoreau also privileges the distant view of the landscape, but in his work this view usually achieves its favored position through a much slower and more deliberate process of comparison and contrast with other views—through a process of contextualization and "composition" not unlike that of the visual artist. And, in any case, the dissolution of the landscape's particular features dramatized in Emerson's passage is entirely uncharacteristic of Thoreau, both in his Journal and in his other writings.

This difference suggests why Thoreau's natural description invites richer, more convincing comparisons with luminist painting than do Emerson's more theoretical writings about nature.[30] Emerson has much to say about nature's inspiriting powers, and his intense preoccupation with light and optics has given rise to several important speculations about his influence on luminist painters such as Fitz Hugh Lane and Martin Johnson Heade.[31] But when we examine the actual picture of the world that emerges from the pages of Thoreau's Journal, we find a "structure" that answers with much greater fidelity to the horizontal frameworks of luminist paintings than does Emerson's.

These compositions rarely contain overtly symbolic elements such as the melodramatic skies and promontories in some of Thomas Cole's paintings; rather, they focus our vision on objects in the near or middle distance, which are rendered in hard, exacting detail, even as an intensely spiritual light pervades the surrounding landscape. This light emanates not from a heavenly source above the scene but usually from a sun painted within the dominant horizontal plane of the picture's surface. Often, the medium that generalizes and extends this sunlight is mist or fog, which serves not only to stabilize the vision (adding to

Fitz Hugh Lane, *Ship "Starlight" in the Fog,* 1860. The Butler Institute of American Art, Youngstown, Ohio.

Martin Johnson Heade, *The Stranded Boat,* 1863. Gift of Maxim Karolik for the M. and M. Karolik Collection of American Paintings, 1815–1865. Courtesy, Museum of Fine Arts, Boston.

the striking tranquility of such paintings) but to emphasize the landscape's lateral relations.

Works such as Lane's *Ship "Starlight" in the Fog* (1860) or Heade's *The Stranded Boat* (1863) depict fog as a visually undifferentiated, mediating substance, linking various points along the painting's horizontal plane to one another. In Thoreau's Journal, fog often has exactly this mediating, relational effect (as do some of his other favorite atmospheric conditions, such as smoke and mist). A passage written on July 25, 1852, describes "a perfect sea [of fog] over the great Sudbury meadows," and what impresses Thoreau most about this striking scene is its "levelling" effect: "What levelling on a great scale is done thus for the eye!" (*J*, 4:255, 256).

Yet, the fog in this scene does more than broaden perspective. As in luminist paintings, it also highlights the landscape's most dominant features: "The fog rises highest over the channel of the river and over the ponds in the woods which are thus revealed— I clearly distinguish where white pond lies by this sign"; "I see great wreaths of fog far NE revealing the course of the river"; "I can gage thus pretty accurately what hills are higher . . . by their elevation above the surface of the fog." Even as the fog has the effect of "concealing trees & forests & hills," thus spiritualizing them, it also reveals with striking clarity the actual terrain in which they lie hidden. Furthermore, by causing "the river [to be] elevated," it reveals the geologic past, showing "the ghost of the ample stream that once flowed to ocean between these now distant uplands in another geological period" (*J*, 4:256, 255, 256, 256, 255).*

The Herbert Gleason photograph that illustrates a June 1853 description of fog from the 1906 edition of the Journal (*J*, 5:facing 216) is remarkably true to Thoreau's horizontal vision of nature and to that of luminist painters such as Lane. Lane's use of ruled grids to achieve his haunting effects[32] suggests Thoreau's role as a surveyor of the land-

---

*Another visually undifferentiated substance that, paradoxically, reveals the landscape to Thoreau is snow. For example, see his description of it as "a great revealer" (*J*, 6:124) in an entry made on February 16, 1854.

Herbert W. Gleason, *Fog, from Nawshawtuct Hill, Concord; August 23, 1900.* The Herbert W. Gleason Collection.

scape—as an artist who could see and measure the actual world even as it became spiritualized for him. His careful measuring of the Pond in *Walden* should be read with this in mind.

On September 4, 1851, Thoreau implicitly states the emerging imperative of his Journal's enterprise:

> Improve the opportunity to draw analogies. There are innumerable avenues to a perception of the truth. Improve the suggestion of each object however humble—however slight & transient the provocation—what else is there to be improved? Who knows what opportunities he may neglect. It is not in vain that the mind turns aside this way or that. Follow its leading—apply it whither it inclines to go. Probe the universe in a myriad points. Be avaricious of these impulses. You must try a thousand themes before you find the right one—as nature makes a thousand

acorns to get one oak. He is a wise man & experienced who has taken many views— To whom stones & plants & animals and a myriad objects have each suggested something—contributed something. [*J*, 2 : 457]

Though this passage does not specifically mention the Journal as the register of the perceiver's "many views"—the template on which these views would find their relation—the document's characteristically open form and provisional nature made it the perfect vehicle for a "mind turn[ing] aside this way or that."

On the following day, Thoreau generalized his recent thinking: "All perception of truth is the detection of an analogy" (*J*, 2 : 463). And on September 7, in a passage that probes the question of "How to get the most life," he likens himself to the honeybee, "searching the live long day for the sweets of nature" and asks rhetorically, "Do I not impregnate & intermix the flowers produce rare & finer varieties by transferring my eyes from one to another?" (*J*, 2 : 470). This transferring of the eyes from one object or scene to another is the central action of the perceiving self as Thoreau's Journal reveals it in the 1850s. Much earlier in his career, he had found the directive for this action in Emerson's *Nature*, where his mentor had written that "man is an analogist, and studies relations in all objects" (*CW*, 1 : 19). But now, as with so many other matters, he was prepared to give this activity his own distinctive application.[33]

The Journal's endlessly repeated use of the construction "this reminds me of that" suggests how deeply analogical Thoreau's imagination was. He was attuned to the recognition of visual relation, and was delighted when he found it: "They [seeds] looked just like dense umbrels of white flowers, and in this light, three or four rods off, were fully as white as white apple blossoms. It is singular how one thing thus puts on the semblance of another" (November 7, 1858: *J*, 11 : 293). It seems to have been virtually impossible for him to make an observation of the natural world without comparing it to another—without immediately placing it in the context of a co-lateral image. The resulting pair of images would constitute an analogy or—in a sense different from what Emerson intended by this term—a "correspondence."

Laurence Stapleton goes too far when she says that Thoreau's "love of correspondence" (the observation of visual likeness) has "nothing in common with the Platonizing theory of correspondences of which Emerson is the exponent."[34] Both kinds of correspondence serve a vision of nature spiritualized. But Stapleton's emphasis is correct; Thoreau's characteristic use of the word "correspondence" in his Journal does not imply the relation between inner and outer realities that it does for Emerson. Typical of Thoreau's use of the term is a passage from a Journal entry of November 8, 1858, where he notes that "[c]orresponding to the clouds in the sky are those mazes now on the earth" (*J*, 11:295). He was acutely interested in aesthetic correspondences of this kind, as shown by the following passage recorded on September 4, 1851:

> As I look back up the stream from . . . near the bridge . . . I on the RR. I saw the ripples sparkling in the sun—reminding me of the sparkling icy fleets which I saw last winter—and I saw how one *corresponded* to the other—ice waves to water ones—the erect ice flakes were the waves stereotyped. It was the same sight—the reflection of the sun sparkling from a myriad slanting surfaces at a distance—a rippled water surface or a crystalized frozen one. [*J*, 2:459; emphasis added]

In this passage, correspondence is a process of "reminding," a cross-referencing of the immediate object and an image stored in memory. The phrase "reminds me" (including its close variants) receives extraordinarily heavy use in Thoreau's Journal—it appears at least once in virtually every extended passage of landscape description written in the 1850s—and it almost always suggests both bringing to mind (focusing attention) and calling forth from memory. It describes the activity of immediate observation *and* the activity of providing a context for that observation through comparison. "Reminding" is, in this sense, both a spatial and a temporal process, but either way, it is grounded in the horizontal framework of the natural world rather than in the vertical framework of transcendence.

The passage above, where the phrase "reminds me" signals a relation of likeness, is characteristic of Thoreau in another way: though visual relations of other kinds (contrast or contiguity, for example) have a place in his aesthetic of nature, the overwhelming majority are based on similitude—in this case the similar configuration of waves and ice formations. The dominance of such relations suggests that in his Journal Thoreau was systematically searching the world for likeness, toward the discovery of its larger "symmetry."

It is equally important to notice in this passage that the correspondence it recognizes between water phenomena of summer and winter ("ice waves to water ones") is purely visual ("the same *sight*") rather than organic. Thoreau is not describing scientific phenomena but an appearance of similitude—a "stereotype." And while he sometimes uses his Journal to investigate organic (biological, geologic, or botanical) relationships among natural objects, the greatest number of its recorded observations of similitude are, like the one above, achieved purely through visual means. When Thoreau asks himself, in the spring of 1858, "Does not this gossamer answer to that of the fall?" he is comparing two phenomena of the same general class and, presumably, of similar organic causes; yet what "highlight[s]" the analogy between them, for him, are their "gleaming and waving in the sun, the light flashing along them as they wave in the wind" (March 28, 1858: *J*, 10:327).

The point is even more clearly illustrated by passages in which Thoreau links objects of distinctly different classes (animals and plants, for example) according to some visual aspect, such as a common color or background. In a typical Journal entry, written on January 18, 1859, he describes a rock that "looked like a seal or walrus" (*J*, 11:406) because of the mist that envelops and reconfigures it. Many years earlier, in an entry of August 6, 1853, he wrote: "Do not the flowers of August and September generally resemble suns & stars? (sunflowers & asters and the single flowers of the golden rod)" (*J*, 5:355).

Observations like these, of which there are hundreds in the Journal, demonstrate Thoreau's instinctive recognition of likeness. Yet, taken together with all the other instances of such recognition, they work beyond mere predilection toward a larger conceptual purpose: To witness the visual affinity between the sunflower and the sun is to confirm the relation between the small and the large, the near and the far, the familiar and the unfamiliar (or, rather, to draw the unfamiliar within the realm of the familiar), and ultimately to dramatize the harmony of the cosmos.

Thoreau's often-expressed love of reflections serves this purpose, as a Journal passage written on October 6, 1851, suggests:

> As we paddled down the stream with our backs to the moon, we saw the reflection of every wood & hill on both sides distinctly These *answering* reflections—shadow to substance,—impress the voyager with a sense of *harmony & symmetry*—as when you fold a blotted paper & produce a regular figure.— a dualism which nature loves. [*J,* 3:51; emphases added]

Every observation of this kind in the Journal, no matter how apparently trivial or casually made, works to the same end as does the reflecting surface of the Pond in *Walden:* to dramatize nature's "harmony & symmetry."

Late in his career, Thoreau offered in his Journal a hypothesis that describes his own most characteristic visual procedure: "I suspect that such are the laws of light that our eye, as it were, leaps from one prominence to another, connecting them by a straight line when at a distance and making one side balance the other" (July 16, 1858: *J,* 11:52). Whatever its basis in modern perceptual theory, the things to notice about this observation are the "connecting" and "balance" that result from the eye's leaping from one point to another. Relation and harmony—these are the desiderata of the sauntering eye, the twin objectives of the Journal's unending work, and the central aesthetic values of its picture of the world.

To say that Thoreau depends primarily on visual relations to confirm the harmony of the cosmos implies that, for him, the appearance of the world reveals the deepest structures of reality. From one point of view, this confidence reflects nineteenth-century romanticism's equation of truth and beauty—what is manifest cannot fail to disclose to the poet's eye nature's supernal truths. From another point of view, however, Thoreau's unusually strong commitment to appearance, as an avenue to truth, distinguishes him from the high literary and intellectual romanticism of American culture at mid-century. In an age obsessed with the possible discrepancy between appearance and reality—and, like Ahab, searching nature for what lies "behind" it—Thoreau grounded his search for meaning in what he actually could *see*.

But the kind of relational seeing that revealed truth to Thoreau was, as we have observed, not ordinary perception. Nor was it the specialized perception of the scientist (or even of the naturalist, narrowly defined). Where the latter would look for differences between the gossamer of spring and that of fall, Thoreau's aesthetic eye seeks likeness and symmetry. Aesthetic perception challenges the objectivity of the scientist, who finds truth only in narrowly focused and particularized views of nature. This is part of what Thoreau means when he speaks, in a Journal entry of August 18, 1854, of scientific procedure as "murder," as a dissembling, destructive activity "inconsistent with the poetic perception" (*J*, 6:452). This view is at the heart of his often-stated distinction between "science" and "poetry" as opposing modes of apprehension.

As Nina Baym points out, Thoreau's suspicion of science is a development of the 1850s (a period, paradoxically, when his empirical study of nature intensified) and represents a departure from his earlier faith in it as an avenue to truth.[35] Yet, ever since William Ellery Channing coined the hyphenated phrase that forms the subtitle of his book *Thoreau: The Poet-Naturalist* (1873), many students of Thoreau have tended to understand "poetry" and "science" as fully complementary spheres of endeavor in his life. Modern scholars have supported and refined this view by reminding us that the rigid dichotomy between "two cultures" of our time was not characteristic of Thoreau's era, and that "natural science" in the mid-nineteenth century was an integrated and coherent field.[36] And it has long been recognized that Thoreau, no less than Emerson or Whitman, saw sciences like geology and astronomy as verifying rather than contradicting his sense of an organic universe.

Nonetheless, in certain important respects science and poetry were indeed separate and discontinuous for Thoreau, especially after 1850 and in the period of the mature Journal. On February 18, 1852, for example, he writes: "It is impossible for the same person to see things from the poet's point of view and that of the man of science" (*J,* 3: 311). The fact that Thoreau kept two separate "commonplace books" (both begun around 1850), one for "facts" and the other for "poetry," illustrates the depth of the dichotomy, even if he found the distinction "difficult always to preserve" (February 18, 1852: *J,* 3: 311).

For Thoreau, then, science could lead to a dangerously partial view of reality, in which nature's elements might be pulled out of their relation:

> Science is inhuman. Things seen with a microscope begin to be insignificant. So described, they are as monstrous as if they should be magnified a thousand diameters. Suppose I should see and describe men and houses and trees and birds as if they were a thousand times larger than they are! With our prying instruments we disturb the *balance and harmony* of nature. [May 1, 1859: *J,* 12: 171; emphasis added]

But to view nature aesthetically is to preserve its "balance and harmony" and thereby to perceive its deeper moral and metaphysical coherence. Aesthetic vision in Thoreau is thus a way of knowing more comprehensive than the way of science, and his Journal may be viewed as the record of a lifelong epistemological search. At a deeper level, however, this quest is not only for knowledge but for Truth—for an all-encompassing understanding of "cosmos." We may say, therefore, that Thoreau's Journal enacts a metaphysical quest by developing an epistemology that realizes itself (makes itself available to us) as an aesthetic—as a poetic of space. This formulation is the complex basis for Thoreau's understanding of the moral function of art, and it also is the basis for the Journal's significance as an evolving aesthetic of nature.

Given such a formulation, we can see why Thoreau became impatient with such theoreticians as Gilpin and Ruskin whose studies seemed to define an aesthetic of nature merely in pictorial terms. Only six months after his initial, enthusiastic reading of Gilpin, he says of him: "I wish he would look at scenery sometimes not with the eye of an artist. It is all side screens and fore screens—and near distances—& broken grounds with him" (August 6, 1852: *J*, 4:283). Several years later, upon reading Ruskin's *Modern Painters,* he wrote: "I am disappointed in not finding it a more out-of-door book. . . . He does not describe Nature as Nature, but as Turner painted her, and though the work betrays that he has given a close attention to Nature, it appears to have been with an artist's and critic's design" (October 6, 1857: *J*, 10:69).[37] This judgment is enormously unfair to Ruskin, whose search for nature's meaning—especially its "symmetry"—was in many respects as deeply probing as Thoreau's.* But it emphasizes the degree to which Thoreau wanted more than pictorial effects from his visualizations of nature.

Thoreau's aesthetic thus opposes not only the scientific view of nature but also the "artistic" view, as his age commonly understood it. The latter often resulted in mere "poesy," in a distanced (alienated) "appreciation" of beauty that, like the science of his day, had its foundation in eighteenth-century empiricism. (Gilpin's work, for example, was securely founded on the sensationalism of John Locke.) But opposition does not sufficiently define Thoreau's effort. In his Journal, he is creating, day by day, a new mode of apprehension that mediates between science and art, between "naturalism" and "poetry." Character-

---

*Ruskin's writings certainly reinforced and refined Thoreau's own ideas on nature's symmetry, its "likeness" of forms. Consider, for example, the following passage from Ruskin's *The Elements of Drawing,* which Thoreau read soon after its publication in 1857: "Symmetry, or the balance of parts or masses in nearly equal opposition, is one of the conditions of treatment under the law of Repetition. For the opposition, in a symmetrical object, is of like things reflecting each other: it is not the balance of contrary natures (like that of day and night), but of like natures or like forms; one side of a leaf being set like the reflection of the other in water" (*The Elements of Drawing; in Three Letters to Beginners* [New York: Smith, Elder, 1857], 164).

istically, he drifts back and forth between these poles (for they were the dichotomous categories his era provided him, just as the vocations his era provided him were "naturalist" and "poet"), yet all the while seeking a space of consciousness that lies integrally apart from them and that balances the claims of outer and inner life. The structure that would contain and preserve this balance is what I call his aesthetic of nature.

WILLOWS SHINING IN THE SPRING SUN:
THE REALITY OF PHENOMENA

To say that Thoreau's apprehension of nature's relations is primarily visual—and therefore, in his terms, moral and metaphysical—raises the question of just where these relations exist: in nature as an objective reality or in the mind of the perceiver. From one point of view, Thoreau's relational seeing can be understood as an aspect of romanticism's empowerment of consciousness, because, potentially, it displaces meaning from the objects of sight and reinvests it in the act of perceiving them. Meaning, in this view, inheres in the perceived relation between objects, which is to say, in the mind that makes the relation.

Like the concept of nature as symbol, with which it is closely related, the subjectivism that underlies this view came to Thoreau from Emerson, especially from those parts of Emerson's work (such as the closing sections of *Nature*) that articulate a position very close to that of philosophical idealism. Less directly, it is a legacy of Immanuel Kant, whose *Critique of Judgement* (1790) located the paradigms of aesthetic form in the human mind and *dis*located them from the world. Still more distantly, it takes its impetus from Western philosophers ranging back from Descartes to Plato.[38]

The large question for someone who, like Thoreau, was an inheritor of philosophical idealism but who vividly experienced the world's material presence, was whether nature's perceived visual relations are discovered or created—composed by the seeing eye or inherently "composite." Sometimes Thoreau makes claims as aggressive as the early

Emerson for the capacity of the imperial imagination to "create" the world. On October 26, 1857, for example, he writes in his Journal: "The seasons and all their changes are in me. I see not a dead eel or floating snake, or a gull, but it rounds my life and is like a line or accent in its poem. *Almost* I believe the Concord would not rise and overflow its banks again, were I not here" (*J*, 10:127). Yet, for our purposes, the most important word in this passage is the one to which I have given emphasis: "Almost." It reminds us that, for Thoreau, the world and its structures had an undeniable reality apart from their relation to the human mind.[39]

The delicate balance Thoreau maintains between the creative imagination and the integrity of the world's own structures is evident in an entry of February 9, 1852, made in a period when he was experimenting intensely with landscape perspectives: "A man goes to the end of his garden inverts his head and does not know his own cottage. The novelty is in us, and it is also in nature" (*J*, 3:292). The first sentence, with its image of the head inverted to achieve a defamiliarization (and thus imaginative possession) of the landscape, derives from Emerson. But the second sentence, with its qualification that the "novelty" inheres in the landscape itself, as well as in the perceiver, is distinctively Thoreau's. A great deal of the Journal's work is devoted to balancing these claims, for, unlike the early Emerson, Thoreau was not willing at any stage of his career to grant full supremacy to the imagination.

This remains true even when he is being most self-consciously the artist of the landscape, shaping and composing it with the mind's eye, as in the following entry of October 7, 1857: "[sitting] on the high bank at the east end of Walden this afternoon, at five o'clock, I saw, *by a peculiar intention or dividing of the eye,* a very striking subaqueous rainbow-like phenomenon" (*J*, 10:74; emphasis added; cf. *J*, 10:91). For all the visual manipulation that this passage communicates, Thoreau is not claiming to have created this striking phenomenon; rather, his peculiar intention of the eye has revealed a structure that somehow was already configured by nature and awaiting discovery by the human perceiver.

As this passage suggests, the term that Thoreau most often uses to reconcile the power of the creative eye with the independent status of the world is "phenomenon." Almost any of the Journal's hundreds of uses of this word show that, for him, it means neither the natural object itself nor the mental image of the object in the mind (a dichotomy of Lockean origin to which he does not subscribe), but rather a merging of the two. Nor does Thoreau use the word in the way Emerson typically does: to denote an object of perception secondary to "Reality," a reflected world of "mere" phenomena. A phenomenon for Thoreau is an entity that bridges the gap between subject and object; it is the "structure" that holds this dichotomy together and preserves the world from Emerson's (and, indeed, his own) overreaching romantic imagination. The following passage shows a characteristic use of the term: "The fall of these withered leaves after each rude blast, so clean and dry that they do not soil the snow, is a phenomenon quite in harmony with the winter" (January 31, 1856: *J*, 8:155).

The first thing to notice about this scene is its composite nature. We have here not one leaf but many, and leaves that are described as existing in a particular setting (snow), season (winter), and set of conditions ("withered," "clean," and falling periodically in the wind). While this scene has more elements than some depicted in the Journal, it is nevertheless true that phenomena for Thoreau necessarily are composite; they are contextualizations, unified sets of coherent visual relations.

The mature Journal of the 1850s gathers phenomena, which together form its picture of the world—a picture created by elements that are themselves composite. In this way, the Journal's repeated descriptions of phenomena have the implicit purpose of saving from the Emersonian imperial consciousness *and* from an evolving scientific naturalism a middle level of response that involves both observation and reflection but, in the end, is different from both. A phenomenon is not merely an invention of the imagination ("fancy," the material for "poesy") but has an almost empirical status lying halfway between subjective and objective reality. It is, we may say, the meeting place of the perceiver and the perceived. Put another way, a phenomenon is the structure that makes and secures a place for the human response that, in the terms we have defined, is specifically aesthetic.

As the basic elements of Thoreau's picture of the world, phenomena were thus of the greatest importance to him. They structured his world. Perhaps because they were so important, he seems not to have allowed himself very often to question their ontological status, even though many of them—in their very nature—are highly evanescent, even ephemeral, in quality. (Some of those to which he was most often and compellingly drawn, such as frostwork or "gossamer," were dependent for their effects on precise qualities of light and shade, as well as the objects' own delicacy of structure.) For the most part, Thoreau serenely goes about his business of recording his perceptions of phenomena day by day, season by season, year by year. Yet occasionally, as in the following Journal entry of March 16, 1856, we hear a curiously defensive note: "There is, at any rate, such a phenomenon as the willows shining in the spring sun, however it is to be accounted for" (*J*, 8 : 209). In the opening and closing phrases of this sentence, we glimpse a large, unresolved issue in Thoreau's work: though phenomena were forcefully present to his imagination, he had no well-developed perceptual theory or philosophical perspective with which to validate their being. And, at some level, he knew this.

The above passage expresses Thoreau's frustration at being unable to authenticate the reality of a set of visual relations he calls "willows shining in the spring sun" or, by implication, of any such phenomenon. Had he lived closer to the turn of the century, Thoreau would have found in the thought of William James a convincing rationale. Working from the assumptions of early pragmatism, James argued that *"any kind of relation experienced must be accounted as 'real' as anything else in the system."* Not only are relations as real as things, James continued, they *are* things. To deny their integrity and their palpable reality in the perceptual field of the space-time continuum is to deny reality itself.[40]

This point was also made, with equal force, in the early twentieth century by Ernest Fenollosa, who, in his essay, "The Chinese Written Character as a Medium for Poetry" (1916), argued that "[r]elations are more real and more important than the things which they relate." This claim, as Herbert Schneidau has written, was of immense importance

to Ezra Pound in his early, imagist phase, for it gave Pound a rationale
for an "objectivist" poetry. Of special significance to Pound was the
part of Fenollosa's argument that said "primitive [natural] metaphors
do not spring from arbitrary subjective processes. They are possible
only because they follow objective lines of relations in nature herself."
This deepened and confirmed for Pound a distinction he had made
earlier, between "true metaphor . . . or image" and "untrue, or orna-
mental metaphor." True metaphors followed nature's own "lines of relation," whereas "untrue metaphors" emanated from the poet's subjective inner life and were merely decorative.[41]

To speak in these terms brings to mind the extraordinary difference
between Thoreau's formal verse, so much given to the idealization that
Pound associated with "untrue metaphor," and the lyrical, presentational "poetry" of his Journal's prose. The valley that forms the setting
of his poem, "Rumors from an Aeolian Harp," for example, is entirely
metaphorical, "a vale which none hath seen / Where foot of man has
never been" (*CP,* 53). Many of Thoreau's poems, like this one, use aspects of the physical world purely as metaphors for spiritual experience. All this means, of course, is that his formal verse belongs inextricably to his age, which, especially in America, was devoted to
the Ideal.

But the "poetry" of his Journal, like so many other aspects of this
document, often seems to us strikingly modern. One can find within it
many passages whose imagery and rhythms have an almost uncanny
resemblance to imagist poems of the early twentieth century. The following sentence stands on its own as a separate, concluding paragraph
to Thoreau's Journal entry for July 18, 1851, to which it is otherwise unrelated. I will set it in verse, but without altering it in any other respect:

> I first heard the locust sing
> so dry & piercing
> by the side of the pine woods
> in the heat of the day.   [*PJ,* 3:313]

Perhaps it is the early Williams rather than Pound who comes most
immediately to mind here, but the features of poetic language that we

associate with imagism are unmistakable: direct treatment of the objective "thing" or experience, economy of language, and a rhythm of natural musicality rather than that of the metronome.[42] There are hundreds of such sentences in the Journal, many of them, like this one, totally discrete—suggesting that, at some level, Thoreau himself understood them as poetic utterances. It is worth noting, as well, that the intensifier "so," which begins the second line, is one of the most often-repeated words in the Journal. Its effect here, and virtually everywhere it appears, is to emphasize the primary, defining, phenomenological qualities of the thing in itself.

In its minimalist, focused treatment of a natural phenomenon, this "poem" bears a relationship to the Japanese haiku (which was a model for imagist poets) and suggests that the orientalism of Thoreau's thought, usually treated exclusively in thematic terms, has a formal dimension as well. Stephen Owen's studies of Chinese poetry can illuminate this discussion, for Owen makes a fundamental distinction between the way in which Western and Eastern poets employ the images of the natural world. "[I]n the Chinese tradition of reading," Owen writes, "the meaning of a poem as a whole is usually not taken as metaphorical. . . . [T]he reader's first allegiance is to direct presentation of the physical world: when there is a 'blossom-fragrance-stream' 芳泉 in an occasional poem, the reader understands a real stream filled with the scent of fallen blossoms rather than the metaphorical 'stream' of fragrance blowing through the air."[43]

For Owen, it is in the very nature of Western poets' use of metaphor to arrogate the importance of mind over world, because metaphor always displaces and subordinates the thing it represents; metaphor, in his view, is "the great substitution trope of western poetics."[44] Unlike Western poetry, classical Chinese poetry is not heavily dependent on metaphor. Instead, it employs a mode of representation Owen calls "parallelism": "Parallelism and metaphor are essentially different: unlike metaphor, parallelism supposes that both terms are present on the same level of discourse and that neither 'stands in for' the other. Metaphor subordinates its terms: one points to the other (whether it is known or not). Parallelism is content to let its terms rest side by side."

In poems structured by parallelism, "[r]elations are 'discovered' or intuitively sensed in the things themselves; they are not presented as the poet's assertions." [45]

Thoreau's Journal is not a poetic "text" in quite the same sense as the works treated in Owen's study. But his heavy use of visual analogy in landscape description strongly suggests the process Owen calls parallelism. In fact, an entry of November 28, 1856, shows Thoreau using Owen's exact term in observing "a marked parallelism" between reflected sunlight on twigs and "lines of gossamer at this season, being almost exactly similar to the eye" (*J*, 9:140). The force of such parallelisms in the Journal is to bring both objects being compared vividly before our eyes, giving priority to neither, and drawing no special attention to the viewer's act of perception.

It would be a mistake, however, to apply Owen's distinction broadly to the procedures of Thoreau's Journal. As a romantic writer, Thoreau is often given to the traditional use of metaphor even in this document. Indeed, the Journal includes many passages that very self-consciously (artfully) extend a controlling metaphor page after page. [46] Such passages compel our attention toward the mind making (creating) its relations and remind us strongly of the conceits of seventeenth-century metaphysical poets, whose works deeply influenced Thoreau.

But Owen's distinction is useful because it suggests an important tendency in Thoreau's thought. Parts of his Journal, especially those parts devoted to landscape description, strive toward an objectivist, presentational view of the world. And this is true, often, even when he is employing metaphor. The following sentence, from an entry of September 11, 1853, is instructive: "In a stubble field I go through a very fine diffusely branching grass now going to seed, which is like a reddish mist to my eyes—2 feet deep—& trembling around me" (*J*, 5:423).

Technically, this imagery ("like a reddish mist to my eyes") is metaphoric, but the sentence's aggregating phrases give the mist a vivid ("trembling") life of its own. The result is that both terms, the grass and the mist, seem to predicate each other. And we know that, on another occasion tomorrow or the next day, Thoreau may well perceive in the landscape a reddish mist that *itself* could become the immediate subject of his vision. That is, the context of the Journal (and the activity of journal-writing) implicitly gives materiality to an image that otherwise would be merely metaphoric. In this case, as in many others in the Journal, we experience the metaphoric relation not as displacement but as placement. The relation belongs to imagination, but it also belongs to the world.

The point I wish to make is that all the forms of comparison that Thoreau employs in landscape description, including metaphor and analogy, potentially belong to the larger relational force of his imaginative life. The figures he employs are sometimes conventional and sometimes strikingly original, even "modernist." But always they reveal a mind given endlessly to connecting the things of this world.

The dominance of such figures in the Journal helps to explain the particular quality of its lyricism. When its multitude of comparisons are considered as a totality, they sing a chorus of relation. This is the chorus of which we hear a part in the climactic chapter of *Walden*, "Spring," where Thoreau's relational imagination tumbles from one likeness to another as he describes the railroad cut in the thaw: "the sand begins to flow like lava. . . . As it flows it takes the forms of sappy leaves or vines . . . , resembling, as you look down on them, the laciniated lobed and imbricated thalluses of some lichens; or you are reminded of coral, of leopards' paws or birds' feet, of brains or lungs or bowels, and excrements of all kinds" (305; cf. *J*, 6:148–49). This vision of interrelatedness continues in the paragraphs that follow, as Thoreau finds in the "feathers and wings of birds . . . still drier and thinner leaves" and sees in "the lumpish grub in the earth . . . the airy and fluttering butterfly" (306).

The difference between the presentational poetry of some of Thoreau's Journal prose and his conventional, idealizing verse reminds us that, for all the incipient modernism of his thought, he belonged largely to his time. Philosophical idealism was inevitably his legacy. But what makes him so interesting to us is that he inherited idealism not as a faith but as a problem. His intense love of the sentient world of things, his profound reluctance to leave things behind even as he tried to view them symbolically, drove him toward strategies of perception and language that anticipate twentieth-century poetry and thought. In the living practice of his Journal, he stands on the threshold of an objectivist, process-oriented philosophy.

But in his conceptualizations of mind and world, Thoreau remains trapped within the intellectual framework of his time. The twin axioms of idealism and dualism could not rescue him from perplexity when he was considering how to justify philosophically the reality of "willows shining in the spring sun." Lacking a rationale for the ontological status of relations, and of the "phenomena" they constitute, all he can do is insist on their reality, rather like Doctor Johnson kicking the stone.

That Thoreau exhibits awareness of this problem only occasionally in his Journal is the result, in part, of the essential privacy of the document, whose unresolved issues never surface for public scrutiny, except as they find their way (reformulated through revision and synthesis) into his published works. Thoreau's only obligation in his Journal, where the artful synthesis of form and idea was not requisite, was to faithfully record perceptions and sometimes his immediate reflection upon them. In such a context, Thoreau was free, like Whitman in his own loosely structured "catalogues" of experience, to contradict himself. A philosophical rationale for the ontological status of phenomena is always just around the corner in the Journal. As a matter of procedure, Thoreau is never called upon for the resolution of this or any other issue.

From another point of view, however, Thoreau does provide a rationale for the ontological status of "willows shining in the spring sun." In saying, "There *is,* at any rate, such a phenomenon" (emphasis added), he asserts an experiential test for reality and in this sense can be said to anticipate the work of James and other objectivist philosophers of the twentieth century. Something so vividly seen, so unmistakably "presenced" before the eyes, must be real. Thoreau believed that the implied, imagined reader of his Journal could not fail to be convinced, by his vivid descriptions of phenomena rendered over and over again—at their appointed time in the annual round, through years of time—of their certain reality. The act of repetition was itself his proof, and the essential work of the Journal was to draw and re-draw the world of phenomena with such thoroughness that in the end it would offer a full spectrum of views—overwhelming in its testamentary power.

A little more than a year after the publication of *Walden,* Thoreau wrote about the Pond: "Of course, if there were eyes enough to occupy all the east shore, the whole pond would be seen as one dazzling shimmering lake of melted gold" (October 19, 1855: *J,* 7 : 499). The impossible condition premised here—not only that the shore would be lined with eyes, but that all these eyes would act as one—is what the Journal seeks to achieve through the perception of one endlessly patient observer. Thoreau's implicit goal in the Journal is to overcome the human limitations of this single observer by gleaning phenomena from thousands of discrete observations and integrating them into a comprehensive vision of reality. If Walden's shore were lined with a thousand eyes, and if another several thousand were clustered on the overlying hills, their composite vision would achieve in an instant what the Journal strives for in gathering in the myriad discrete observations of a lifetime.

The unstated assumption of the Journal is that at some future point, a point always receding before the endless work of observation, the picture will be complete. At that moment, the master perceiver will collect his views and integrate them into a coherent vision, which would be nothing less than the world as seen in the mind of God. Such a vision is the ultimate purpose of the Journal's picture of the world, and it suggests another way in which Thoreau's aesthetic of nature is at the service of larger epistemological and metaphysical purposes. Hardly the mere compendium of facts that it sometimes has been called, Thoreau's Journal is for him *the* indisputable evidence of nature's reality. To describe, and to describe comprehensively, is to affirm the world's body.

In this sense, the Journal—so open and apparently provisional in form—always awaits closure, which, because of the immensity (and ultimate impossibility) of the task, never comes. Yet, despite its provisional form, the Journal's overriding object is closure. As a document based upon the promise of deferred synthesis, it provides the ideal context for a mind that characteristically divided the activities of observation (whether carried on in a spirit of wonder or of scientific inquiry) and reflection into separate experiences rather than intermixing them. The Journal, in other words, is a work whose form encourages a two-stage process of assimilating nature's truths, with the second stage always necessarily suspended.

Looked at in this way, the charts of natural phenomena that Thoreau drew up near the end of his life may be understood as an utterly inadequate attempt to complete the second stage. Though he himself surely was more ambitious for them than this, they appear in retrospect to merely gesture toward his goal of fully conjoining observation and reflection, of filling out the entire time-space continuum. The fact that these charts have more empty spaces than full ones demonstrates their inadequacy; their incompleteness has far less to do with Thoreau's failing health than with the impossibility of his task.

The problem, of course, is that there will never be enough eyes to see the whole of Walden or enough time in which to see it, much less to gather and synthesize its meanings. (*Walden* itself may be understood as an attempt to accomplish this feat.) But it is the desire rather than the fulfillment that concerns us here. What Thoreau wants from his Journal and its emergent picture of the world is suggested by a Journal passage written on February 3, 1855: "I still recur in my mind to that skate of the 31st. I was thus enabled to get a bird's-eye view of the river,—to survey its length and breadth within a few hours, connect one part (one shore) with another in my mind, and realize what was going on upon it from end to end,—to know the whole as I ordinarily knew a few miles of it only" (*J*, 7:168). This comprehensive, relational vision (an aesthetic vision, because it is relational) is what Thoreau seeks from his Journal.

Two and a half years after Thoreau testified to the certain reality of willows shining in the spring sun, he wrote in his Journal: "I look down a straight reach of water to the hill by Carlisle Bridge,—and this I can do at any season,—the longest reach we have. It is worth the while to come here for this prospect,—to see a part of earth so far away over the water that it appears islanded between two skies. *If that place is real, then the places of my imagination are real"* (August 24, 1858: *J,* 11 : 122; emphasis added). This passage reveals Thoreau's ultimate purpose in attempting to validate the reality of phenomena, and expresses the fullest meaning of "correspondence" for him. In their "imaginative," or "phenomenal," quality, scenes of this kind correspond to inner life, so that in confirming the reality of phenomena, Thoreau is also confirming the reality (and authenticity) of the imagination.

The intimate relation of dreams to "phenomena" is addressed in an entry Thoreau made in the previous year. On October 29, 1857, he argues that "Dreams are real," and that phenomena of a dreamlike nature have "a real basis in my world." In making his case, he identifies a special time "in the early morning hours, when there is a gradual transition from dreams to waking thoughts, from illusions to actualities, as from darkness, or perchance moon and star light, to sunlight": "Such early morning thoughts as I speak of occupy a debatable ground between dreams and waking thoughts. They are a sort of permanent dream in my mind" (*J,* 10:141).

This experience is closely related to the state of being that Thoreau describes in *A Week* when he writes, "Our truest life is when we are in dreams awake" (297). He makes essentially the same effort to establish the reality of dreams as he does to validate the ontological status of phenomena: he seeks to confer authenticity on a level of experience that most people would consider merely transitory or transitional (between sleep and wakefulness), but which for him is integral and revelatory. In another sense of the phrase from *Walden,* this effort is Thoreau's "morning work"—his lifelong work of legitimating the level of experience that phenomena define. The task of his aesthetic, and of his Journal, is to make a place for phenomena to be real.

Morning work is the kind of phenomenological endeavor that, in the twentieth century, Gaston Bachelard would identify with the poetics of reverie—thereby explicitly linking knowing, being, and art in a full privileging of the imagination.[47] For Thoreau, unlike Bachelard, phenomenology was inextricably bound up with phenology—the quasi-scientific classification of natural phenomena according to their seasonal appearance.[48] But the movement from phenology to phenomenology is already profoundly, if only implicitly, at work in Thoreau's writings in a way that cannot be discerned, for example, in the work of Gilbert White and other earlier naturalists. This movement is especially apparent in his Journal, whose open form and spontaneity distinguish it from *A Week* and *Walden;* these works, for all their structural and stylistic idiosyncrasies, were nevertheless "books," "narratives," whose form was shaped, in part, by audience expectation. Among Thoreau's major writings, the Journal is the work in which his incipient modernism is most clearly revealed, and in which his emergent picture of the world can best be viewed.

four

THE
CATEGORICAL
IMAGINATION

T he Journal is the verbal space in which Thoreau's imagination found greatest freedom. Unlike *A Week* and *Walden,* each resulting from years of studied revision, it provided the ideal context for a mind given to immediate and ranging, sometimes extravagant, acts of imaginative connection.* The Journal is a canvas filled with association, its aesthetic eye connecting "one prominence to another" through the continuous activity of visual comparison. As the subject-viewer (the "I" of the Journal) finds, or makes, relation among the landscape's diverse features, he affirms the interrelatedness of the

---

*When viewed against the radically provisional nature of Emerson's Journal, of course, Thoreau's Journal seems deliberate, and Perry Miller used this comparison against Thoreau in claiming that his Journal's method is "dogged" and its "narration as contrived as any in the language" (*Consciousness in Concord,* 23, 26, 108–9). But Thoreau's supple, often lyrical prose simply will not support such a judgment. A more discerning response to his deliberateness is the wonder expressed by Alfred Kazin: "It is not natural for a man to write this well every day" ("Thoreau's Journals," in *Thoreau: A Century of Criticism,* ed. Walter Harding [Dallas: Southern Methodist University Press, 1954], 188).

cosmos, and this affirmation in turn creates a sense of intimacy ("correspondence") between the perceiving self and the world.

In linguistic terms, this activity may be seen as an act of sustained predication, the writer continuously defining the particular objects of his perception by linking them through comparison to a wide variety of other objects that exist within the immediate field of vision or in memory. The result, as we witness it on page after page of the Journal, is an endless elaboration of the natural world through association. So pervasive is the Journal's use of associative constructions that one is tempted to say that Thoreau's imagination is controlled by what Roman Jakobson called the metonymic, as opposed to the metaphoric, pole of language.[1] To argue from such a theoretical position would be to posit a physiological basis for Thoreau's habitual recognition of likeness (Jakobson linked these poles to two distinct forms of aphasia) and to contend that the writer's sense of an interrelated cosmos was a legacy of temperament as much as it was a legacy of Emersonian Transcendentalism. However, we need not commit ourselves to one particular explanation of the Journal's intense predication of the world. What is important to recognize is that, to a degree unusual even for a thinker whose intellectual inheritance commanded a search for interrelatedness, Thoreau is deeply given to imaginative association, and that the Journal offered him the private (meditative), provisional form in which such association could range most widely and freely.

Yet, for all the play of association exhibited in the Journal, it is impossible to sustain a reading of this document without recognizing within it a tendency of exactly opposite effect. Thoreau's relational imagination is like Whitman's spider, forever sending out its filaments to discover new, previously unperceived phenomena. Another force, equally strong, seeks to draw these very phenomena inward toward predetermined categories of perception and cognition—to place and organize them, and thereby to know them.

From one point of view, this second force may be understood as the deductive, classifying, "scientific" part of Thoreau's mind that gives impetus to his many inquiries into botany, forestry, animal life, geology, and anthropology. Yet these terms do not adequately define this force, because the writer's scientific inquiries are themselves characterized not only by classification but also by the same spirit of imaginative exploration as are his "poems." Indeed, some of Thoreau's most important scientific discoveries, such as those relating to the succession of forest trees or to the new species of fish he found in Walden Pond, are as indebted to imaginative association as they are to classification.[2]

Further, the categorizing tendency of the Journal makes itself felt in many areas that cannot, even from the perspective of Thoreau's own time, be considered scientific at all—the classification of landscape views, for example. Even while Thoreau was being severely critical of Gilpin and Ruskin for what he regarded as their arbitrary organization of aesthetic responses, he was himself actively involved for years in the same process, constantly viewing and re-viewing the scenes around Concord in an attempt to place them—often within categories derived directly from these very thinkers.[3] The Journal is, in part, a record of Thoreau's attempt to systematize such views and revise them in accordance with his own perceptions.

The systematizing tendency of the Journal requires a term of definition broader than science, and the one I propose is the categorical imagination. Where Thoreau's relational imagination is exploratory and essentially undirected ("the wild"), the categorical imagination is committed to placement and permanence ("the good"). It always wants to know where it is, and its primary business is marking the boundaries of sensory experience. The categorical imagination wants to structure perception, and the Journal was the most natural context in which this process could occur.

At the most local level, we can observe this process in the hundreds of instances in the Journal where Thoreau spontaneously, impulsively, names what he is experiencing as the dominant feature of a day: "This is a day of sunny water" (Aug. 8, 1854: *J*, 6:429); "It is a turtle day" (May 1, 1859: *J*, 12:172). Naming performed in such a context is an elemental form of categorization, the beginning stage toward abstraction. As Thoreau's naming reaches out to embrace longer spans of time, we can feel him moving toward a more deliberate stage of categorization. On October 11, 1857, reflecting on the "glorious weather" of the previous week, he writes, "Perhaps these might be called Harvest Days"; considering another aspect of the week's phenomena in the same passage, he adds, "These are cricket days" (*J,* 10:86).

But, whether impulsive or studied, such naming is more than a move toward abstraction. It is also a vivid, material characterization, or "presencing," of the temporal unit called a day. That is, in his categorizations Thoreau not only generalizes upon experience; he highlights it, particularizes it, through contextualization. Naming is an act of appropriation, and in Thoreau's case this means not only placing the thing that is named but also emphasizing its very aspect as a "thing"—embodying it, bringing it alive to the imagination. To name phenomena, for Thoreau, was to authenticate their being, and the Journal allowed names to be stored and called up again for their power to confirm the validity of categories. This is the import of a passage written very late in the Journal's development: "You may say that now, when most trees have fully expanded leaves and the black ash fairly shows green, the leafy season has fairly commenced. (I see that I so called it May 31 and 27, 1853)" (June 4, 1860: *J,* 13:329).

While Thoreau's categorizing tendency becomes most recognizable in the late Journal (this has sometimes been cited as a sign of the Journal's failure in its final years) and in the charts of natural phenomena he developed at the end of his life, it manifests itself strongly, if less schematically, during the entire decade of the 1850s. The deeper we probe into Thoreau's Journal of this period, the more we see that one of its most distinctive features is a balancing of the relational and categorical imaginations. Yet we also come to see that, as understood by Thoreau, these forces, while opposites, are not oppositional. Their copresence in the Journal is not a reflection of ambivalence, nor can their relationship be defined in any strict sense as dialectical. Rather, the relationship between relation and category in the mature Journal is most accurately defined as one of reciprocity.

Relations are always perceived, by Thoreau, within categories—within predetermined, cognitive frameworks. These are the embracing designs, the structures, in which creativity proceeds. If "phenomena" are perceived relations between natural objects, then Thoreau's categories are clusters, coherent aggregates, of phenomena. That is to say, they are frameworks of cognition rather than perception and are characterized not by the internal "relations" among discrete objects but by the external (conceptual) boundary that the mind prepares for their reception.

But Thoreau's categories are themselves products of ranging observation and association; they form out of his visual experience and, once formed, become determinants in what he consciously or unconsciously chooses to see. This is part of what Thoreau means when he says, "[Y]ou will not see these splendors, whether you stand on the hilltop or in the hollow, unless you are prepared to see them. The beauty of the earth answers exactly to your demand and appreciation" (November 2, 1858: *J*, 11:278).

The process I am describing belongs to Thoreau's scientific observations no less than to his aesthetic responses: "As usual with the finding of new plants, I had a presentiment that I should find the ledum in Concord. It is a remarkable fact that, in the case of the most interesting plants which I have discovered in this vicinity, I have anticipated finding them perhaps a year before the discovery" (February 4, 1858: *J*, 10:274). To have "anticipated" a discovery is already to have prepared a category for receiving and understanding it, as Thoreau suggests when he says, "We hear and apprehend only what we already half know" (January 5, 1860: *J*, 13:77). Such half-knowledge reflects a visceral process of category-formation. Like Thomas S. Kuhn's "paradigm" or Michael Polanyi's "tacit knowledge," Thoreau's category functions intuitively.[4]

"THE REIGN OF WATER": CATEGORIES EMERGING

On October 27, 1857, Thoreau writes in his Journal: "The reign of water now begins, and how it gambols and revels! Waves are its leaves, foam its blossoms. How they run and leap in great droves, deriving new excitement from each other! Schools of porpoises and blackfish are only more animated waves and have acquired the gait and game of the sea itself" (*J*, 10:130). The extravagant play of association in this

passage—it begins with Concord's watery autumn and reaches outward to the world's vast oceans—is directly dependent on Thoreau's
confidence in the perceptual category, "[t]he reign of water." Yet this
category could never have emerged and consolidated itself as a category without years of observing nature's myriad phenomena.

Moments of perceptual consolidation, when the discrete observations of years leap into formation, are among the most interesting to
observe in the Journal. On September 12, 1851, for example, the writer
suddenly proclaims, "This is the season of fogs" (*J*, 2 : 494). These moments almost always are announced, as here, in strongly declarative
terms, and they occur only when Thoreau is sufficiently certain of his
emergent category to give it a name. Such a statement says, "I now
perceive that these phenomena that I previously saw as diverse, even
unrelated, are dominated by one particular aspect that unifies them
and gives them definition. This is the framework (in visual terms, the
'frame') through which I now see them. This is their essential character." In such moments, we witness the high drama of perception in the
Journal: the sudden awareness of coherence, of "cosmos." The perception that gives rise to the pronouncement "This is the season of fogs"
calls to mind the moment in *Walden* when Thoreau asks, "Walden, is
it you?" (193). Both are moments of recognition and perceptual uni-
fication, a coming into focus of the world—a "worlding," in this sense.

But, as theoreticians of art such as E. H. Gombrich tell us, no
category of perception exists without prior categories, without what
Gombrich calls preexisting "schemata."[5] And one must therefore
imagine that the discrete observations that eventually gave rise to categories like "the reign of water" and "the season of fogs" were themselves products of prior, perhaps highly provisional, categories of perception. So intimate is the Journal's reciprocity of relation and category,
observation and generalization, that it is impossible to say which comes
first in any given instance of perception recorded there. This intimacy
makes Thoreau's category something very different from Kant's, which
exists a priori to our perception of the mobile, diverse, living world.
Thoreau's categories, unlike Kant's, are of the world—they emerge
from it, even as they engender fresh new explorations of the world,

which in turn lead to the creation of still further categories. Categorization in Thoreau is an earth-bound, perceptually grounded process.

That some kind of distance was necessary in one's transaction with the world is something Thoreau knew well, and, as the following Journal passage suggests, he also knew that the habitual failure to achieve this distance could result in disorientation and malaise: "Only the rich and such as are troubled with ennui are implicated in *the maze of phenomena*. You cannot see anything until you are clear of it" (November 1, 1858: *J,* 11:273; emphasis added). Categories for Thoreau, then, are a way of seeing, of gaining the "doubleness and distance" he celebrates in the same Journal passage and also describes in the chapter of *Walden* called "Solitude" (134–35). But in Thoreau's world, unlike Kant's, the category and the world are always sliding back and forth in relation to one another, like a refracting telescope pointing in opposite directions at the same time, constantly shaping and refocusing each other. This is part of what Transcendental "correspondence" meant for Thoreau, as he adapted this term from Emerson for his own distinctive purposes.

The fluid reciprocity between Thoreau's evolving categories and the particular images that find their place within them is one of the most prominent aspects of the Journal as a work of art. One way of measuring the formal success of the writer's natural description is to judge when the balance between relation and category is most fully reciprocal: that is, when the categories are supple and inviting enough to point Thoreau toward a rich particularity of observation, and when, conversely, the individual observations are poignant and original enough to enlarge and refine his categories.

Among Thoreau's works, only the Journal could have accommodated the complex process I am describing. In a more formal text like *Walden,* one that assumed closure, the reciprocity between relation and category could be stated ("I love the wild not less than the good" [*Wa,* 210]) but not fully dramatized, because the full development of this process requires an entirely open-ended temporal framework. In the short run of experience, relation and category, observation and generalization, often appear contradictory; there are numerous instances in the Journal where observations plainly do not fit the category in which Thoreau is attempting to place them or where they resist categorization altogether. But in the Journal, such anomalies could always await another day, another set of observations that might verify or revise present categories.

Another way to state this observation is to say that, as a private document, the Journal never required overt reconciliation of what otherwise might (in discrete moments along the way) have appeared as contradictions between facts and ideas. This is not to say that in his Journal Thoreau does not attempt resolution of such contradictions; there are many passages of broad philosophical import that make this attempt. But such passages, even when they are filled with rhetorical certitude, occur in a context that allows for constant revision. In this larger sense, resolution of conflict between facts and ideas is systematically deferred in the Journal.

We may go further and say that, for Thoreau, the very act of making a "book" implied closure. That *Walden* is the result, literally, of transferring Journal material into a narrative framework is but the most obvious aspect of this implication. To make a book like *Walden* meant drawing a boundary around the experiences it describes. Textuality, as Thoreau and his age understood it, prompted him to think of books in this way, and it is precisely because he did not have to think of his Journal as a text that he felt free to range between category and relation exactly as the power of paradigms, on the one hand, and the power of the world's images, on the other, moved him. Thoreau's Journal called for abstraction only when the spirit called—occasionally, to the occasion—and when facts had sufficiently arranged themselves in his imagination to form a category spontaneously.

When Whitman said, "Do I contradict myself? / Very well then I contradict myself," he was offering one characteristically romantic (and thoroughly Emersonian) solution to the problem of reconciling fact and idea. But this solution is based solely on the ego's transcendence of both fact and idea; it assumes that at the phenomenological, experiential level of reality these terms often exist in apparent contradiction, which can only be reconciled, as in "Song of Myself" or in the final sections of Emerson's *Nature,* by spiraling beyond both. Thoreau's romantic ego is no smaller than Emerson's or Whitman's, but the method of his Journal saved him from the excesses of the imperial imagination. It provided a context in which fact and idea could order themselves laterally, in a relation of relative equality, rather than hierarchically. Not only did the Journal, through its open form, allow this latitude—it created it. Thus, even as the Journal stood as a record of the complex reciprocity between relation and category, fact and idea, observation and generalization, it also served as the instrument through which that reciprocity was perceived, understood, and enacted.

One of the reasons Thoreau's categories could never assume the fully abstracted status of the Kantian category is his acute awareness of and sensitivity to change, and the impact of change on our habitual ways of seeing. On March 19, 1858, he writes:

> These spring impressions (as of the apparent waking up of the meadow described [in the Journal] day before yesterday) are not repeated the same year, at least not with the same force, for the next day the same phenomenon does not surprise us. Our appetite has lost its edge. The other day the face of the meadow wore a peculiar appearance, as if it were beginning to wake up under the influence of the southwest wind and the warm sun, but it cannot again this year present precisely that appearance to me. I have taken a step forward to a new position and must see something else. You perceive, and are affected by, changes too subtle to be described. [*J,* 10:307]

At every moment there is change, refocusing our vision and potentially remaking our categories of perception. This lesson, too, Thoreau learned from his Journal; its discipline required fresh, daily observation and thus kept him ever-attentive to changes both in nature and in himself.

His acute awareness of change did not, however, cause him to abandon himself joyously to the infinite expansion of categories, as it did for Emerson in "Circles." Nor did it lead him to the position toward

which Melville moved in *Moby Dick:* a fateful resignation to the necessary failure of the human imagination to perceive the true categories of
reality. Thoreau's response to the radical subjectivism of high romanticism was not to leap beyond or ignore categories, but to search the
world constantly for categories that were, at least provisionally, viable.
What Thoreau is always seeking—even when his relational imagination ranges most freely—is a structure to contain his explorations of
phenomena, a structure that will, in some sense, sanction that exploration. Thus, relation in Thoreau is associated with change, whereas
category represents a commitment to permanence. His categories are
frameworks (or "frames") for containing and understanding change—
a way of making the world hold still.[6] The mature Journal may be
understood as a search for viable structures of perception, categories
large enough and sufficiently well delineated to encompass any and all
change, even the most subtle.

Sometimes, as on October 14, 1857, Thoreau would "doubt if you
can ever get Nature to repeat herself exactly" (*J*, 10:97). Far more
typically, however, he would search natural phenomena for those
things that did repeat and would thereby allow themselves to be cate-
gorized. Indeed, the search for the "annual" or "constant phenomenon" (November 8 and 26, 1860: *J*, 14: 224, 272), the event whose occurrence was absolutely predictable year to year, becomes ever more
intense as we move deeper into the late Journal. But Thoreau's desire
for certitude is evident at earlier stages as well. On September 6, 1854,
he asked, "Is not all our really hot weather *always* contained between
the 20th of May and the middle of September?" (*J*, 7:17; emphasis
added). A week earlier he posed a question, regarding the appearance
of fog after a change in the weather, that expresses his deepest wish for
certain knowledge of seasonal change: "Is it always so?" (August 30,
1854: *J*, 6:487).

We may say that Thoreau's sense of the provisional aspect of categories was more theoretical than functional. In practice, he believed in
his categories and experienced them as permanent; by the mid-1850s
his procedure of grouping phenomena within them has become rou-
tine. The following sentence from an entry of May 5, 1854, is—in both

import and idiom—characteristic: "Put this [Thoreau's observation of a field] with the grassy season's beginning" (*J*, 6:236). Though Thoreau's Journal necessarily immersed him daily in process, he believed that the structures, the categories, that finally emerged for him out of this process would hold—that they would confirm for him a stable vision of cosmos.*

Thoreau gained much of this confidence from his recognition, in 1852, of the circle of time, for here was the ultimate category that could validate all the others. As the overarching design of his thought, it liberated a mind given to both categorical and relational thinking. The great turning wheel of the seasons, apprehended visually, would always provide an embracing structure for change, and every category, such as "the reign of water," represented a segment along its arc—an arc describing all seasons and everything seasonal. Each category, insofar as it proved itself viable, was, like the circle of time, a coordinate of time and space (the *season* of *fogs*). As much as Walden Pond, a category was a "little world," a microcosm whose unity would mirror the cosmos. We may say that Thoreau's apprehension of the circle of time in 1852 stabilized his search for cosmos, and one reason for his singleminded devotion to his Journal in the 1850s is that this is the open form best suited to that search.

But Thoreau's confidence in his categories was more than conceptual. He earned it from the very practice of keeping his Journal, which showed him how serviceable his emerging categories were, how re-

---

*This point suggests my differences with two key studies of the 1970s, McIntosh's *Thoreau as Romantic Naturalist* (1974) and Garber's *Thoreau's Redemptive Imagination* (1977). These works placed Thoreau in the context of transatlantic romanticism and deepened our sense of the complexity of his thought by showing the range of his attempts to reconcile the demands of self and world. But the Thoreau who emerges from these studies is defined predominantly by "ambivalence" (Garber) and "polarity" or "shiftiness" (McIntosh, 37–38, 68, 77). At many points in Thoreau's work (sometimes, even at the level of the individual sentence), one can indeed find a pattern of "advance and sidestep through which a position is promoted and then qualified" (Garber, 178). But to say that "Thoreau never reaches final conclusions about nature, never attempts to define it" (McIntosh, 46) is to take a good argument too far. Thoreau's mature Journal reveals the consolidation of certain firm structures of perception and belief.

sponsive they were to the world's particularity and changefulness. Though theoretically provisional, Thoreau hardly ever had to abandon them. Rather, he characteristically redrew their boundaries to allow for the fruits of new observation without relinquishing their essential form. In any given year after its formation, the "reign of water" might absorb or eliminate a few particular elements, but the category itself was unshakable. In fact, one of the most clearly recognizable developments in the Journal from about 1850 through its close in 1861 is the confirming of categories, most of which took initial shape in the early years of the decade. From this point of view, the charts (Kalendar) that Thoreau drew up in his final years merely represent a further hardening of lines of demarcation that were already clearly drawn by the time he took pen to drawing paper in 1860.

This hardening may be viewed as an ebbing of the Journal's vitality in its closing years, and readers have noticed (and, generally, been disappointed by) the exhaustive tallying of observations that takes place in this period. In the late Journal, the balance between relation and category becomes unsettled during a time when Thoreau's attention to categorizing, as such, becomes more intense. But in its final years, the Journal expresses another kind of excitement: the drama of consolidation, of assembling the parts of the grand vision, of completing the picture of the world. Though intensely systematic, the late Journal is not mechanical; indeed, it contains some of Thoreau's most supple and lyrical prose. The best analogy for its procedures is not the natural scientist classifying his findings (though classification certainly is a part of it), but the luminist painter brushing color into his carefully measured grid. As witnessed in individual entries, the activity of the late Journal may sometimes appear narrowly scientific. But considered in its broad intentions, it is artistic in the fullest sense.

IMPROVING THE SEASONS: THE JOURNAL AS CALENDAR

Categories such as "the reign of water" and "the season of fogs" are spatial (phenomenological) characterizations of time. When viewed abstractly, they may be seen as minor calendrical units—subcategories

of spring, summer, fall, and winter—but they do not emerge from calendrical time. Rather, they emerge directly from the experience of the
self in nature, from the force of their presence to the imagination. Because they exist as integral perceptual units (as "things") prior to our
temporal ordering of them, they are, in Bachelard's term, "primary." [7]
Only secondarily do they take their place, chronologically, in the calendar. In fact, some of them, such as "the reign of water," are not confined
to a single season, but manifest themselves in two or more seasons. [8]

The relation of such categories to calendrical time is suggested by a
sentence recorded in the Journal on October 16, 1859: "The phenomena of our year are one thing, those of the almanac another" (*J*, 12 : 390).
Here Thoreau is implicitly calling attention to the fact that, for all its
elaboration of the annual cycle with history and prediction, the almanac is fixed by calendrical time. It is overcommitted to a set of abstrac-
tions known as the twelve months and the four seasons, and these ab-
stractions do not necessarily answer to our experience of time. The
traditional calendar may actually impede our involvement in the living
world of phenomena.

Thoreau might have attempted to solve this problem in several ways.
One would have been to reject the traditional calendar entirely—to
abandon spring, summer, fall, and winter—and replace it with his
own smaller-scale, perceptually defined seasons such as the reign of
water, turning these local, purely natural categories into full-fledged
seasons and ordering the annual round exclusively according to their
manifestations. Or, more radically, he might have replaced the whole
idea of seasonal demarcation with pure duration (as in modern, Berg-
sonian conceptions of time). But the philosophical thought of his age
did not prepare him for the latter response, and his own predilections
restrained him from a full-scale, phenomenological restructuring of
the annual cycle. Thoreau's approach to calendrical time is revisionary,
not revolutionary.

The nature of this approach is suggested by the following passage
from a Journal entry of March 1, 1854: "Here is our first spring morning according to the almanac. It is remarkable that the spring of the
almanac and of nature should correspond so closely" (*J*, 6 : 145). This

reaction is really twofold: first, there is the pleasurable surprise that the almanac's predicted onset of spring should have occurred at the same moment as spring's "true" beginning; but, second, there is a quiet, implicit satisfaction that nature's spring should have met the almanac's timetable.

Thoreau's relationship to the traditional calendar is not unlike his relationship to the old histories of New England, such as that of Edward Johnson, which he consults in *A Week*. He is dependent on the calendar for authority (since it provides the inevitable, necessary starting point for any consideration of seasonal change) and is aware that its structure—the quartering of the annual cycle—is not altogether arbitrary. Like the work of "the old naturalists" (*J*, 14:117) of New England, which he praises in a Journal entry of October 13, 1860, its conceptions are the result of earlier, primary visions of time and space.

But Thoreau also knows that the calendar, like Emerson's "tradition," has hardened into a formal and highly abstracted system, and that its present lines of demarcation are arbitrary. As categories of perception, neither the months nor the seasons, traditionally demarcated, are responsive to nature's actual currents of change because they have become distanced from perception, which no longer informs them. The challenge Thoreau felt was to measure "not the absolute [abstractly conceived] time but the true time of the season" (August 21, 1851: *J*, 2:415).

Accordingly, a large part of his work in the Journal is to bring the light of perception to the calendar—literally, to illuminate it. That is, Thoreau wants to make a calendar that restructures, but does not relinquish, the terms and elements of the traditional calendar. Such a restructuring is suggested by this Journal passage from February 9, 1854: "Is not January alone pure winter—? December belongs to the fall—is a wintry November—February to the spring—it is a snowy March" (*J*, 6:112). Freed from the tyranny of chronological time, such a calendar would mark the seasons phenomenologically, according to their actual, observed properties, as in the following passage from August 5, 1854: "The fall, *in fact,* begins with the first heats of July. Skunk-cabbage . . . , etc., appear to usher it in. It is one long acclivity from winter to midsummer and another long declivity from mid-summer to winter" (*J*, 6:421; emphasis added). The following spring, Thoreau asks, "Is it not summer now when the creak of the crickets begins to be general?" (May 30, 1855: *J*, 7:399).

To decide that, "in fact," autumn begins in July and that summer begins in May is to appropriate the role of calendar-maker to oneself by appealing to immediate observation, and thus to challenge the traditional calendar's lines of demarcation. This challenge, of course, is part of a larger claim for the efficacy of individual perception. It reflects Thoreau's (romantic) desire to achieve complete originality, to become the genius of the seasons by ordering them in his own distinctive way.

Even so, Thoreau is also challenging the calendar to a restoration of its own prior efficacy. No matter how arbitrary it has become, its origins lie in some deeper, mythic, and natural marking of time. Underlying Thoreau's endeavor is the belief that the personal, subjective view, charged with the power of imagination, corresponds to a mythic, primary view of seasonal change—that a restoration of the calendar's ancient verity can be achieved through individual perception. Part of his role as nature's timekeeper is to restore an older, "truer," calendar. This is one reason for his acute, sustained interest in the American Indians, who "stood nearer to wild nature than we" (March 5, 1858: *J*, 10:294). It also helps to explain his attraction toward "the early writers of New England, like Josselyn and William Wood": "Certainly that generation stood nearer to nature, nearer to the facts, than this" (January 9, 1855: *J*, 7:108, 109).

Thoreau's faithful adherence to "the facts" should remind us that while his understanding of natural change depends upon the individual human perceiver's subjective, "poetic" apprehension, he is ultimately working toward an objectively verifiable measurement of change. It is a real calendar he is remaking, and its emergent categories receive their validation from firsthand observation. The following passage, from a Journal entry of April 16, 1854, is instructive:

It is remarkable how the American mind runs to statistics. . . .
Every shopkeeper makes a record of the arrival of the first mar-

tin or bluebird to his box. Dodd, the broker, told me last spring
that he knew when the first blue-bird came to his boxes, he
made a memorandum of it: John Brown, merchant, tells me this
morning that the martins first came to his box on the 13th, he
'made a minute of it.' Beside so many entries in their day-books
and ledgers, they record these things. [*J*, 6 : 200]

Who else is Thoreau describing here but himself? Far more than
Dodd or Brown, he is the rigorous observer and chronicler of the her-
alds of spring, and his own daybook—the Journal—is a fuller record
of such phenomena than that of any other Yankee. The "American
mind," so committed to empirical observation and measurement, is
Thoreau's own. The conjunction of the poetic and the empirical, the
subjective and the objective, is one of the most striking features of his
imagination.

The charts Thoreau drew up between 1860 and 1862 (his Kalendar)
are the literal expression and outcome of his effort to create a truer
calendar, but these fragmentary documents are merely a token of what
he was trying to achieve. The Journal itself is the calendar that Thoreau
actually made, and to understand its purposes we must turn to its daily
business of revising the seasons. That Thoreau was engaged in such
revision very early in the 1850s is evident from the following Journal
passage from an entry of October 28, 1852:

> 4 months of the green leaf make all our summer, if I reckon from
> June 1st to Oct 1st—the growing season & methinks there are
> about 4 months when the ground is white with snow[.] That
> would leave two months for spring & 2 for autumn. October the
> month of ripe or painted leaves—Nov. perchance the month of
> withered leaves. [*J*, 4 : 403–4]

We feel here the push toward symmetry—toward conceptualizing the
annual cycle in such a way that the "green" months balance the "white."
In the five-year period after this passage was written, Thoreau continued to reflect in similar ways upon the distinctive features of the
annual cycle. On October 26, 1857, he was prepared to be concise and

definitive: "Spring is brown; summer, green; autumn, yellow; winter, white; November, gray" (*J,* 10:129).

Here the writer apprehends the seasons according to a broad aesthetic category, their prevailing color, gathering their import under a single, ruling term. But what is most interesting about this passage is that the traditional seasons are followed by "November" so automatically, without any qualification or explanation in the surrounding text. In the passage of October 1852, Thoreau had included characterizations of October and November, but only as subcategories of fall ("2 [months] for autumn"). Now, after years of observation, "November" appears to have emerged for him as a distinctively identifiable season of its own. The following year (1858) confirmed the new seasonal status of November: "now a new season begins, the pure November season of the russet earth and withered leaf and bare twigs and hoary withered goldenrods" (November 10, 1858: *J,* 11:306).

Eighteen fifty-eight was the year in which "November" came fully into focus for Thoreau as a seasonal, which is to say, phenomenological, category. He was now certain of its visual integrity and had mastered its constituent elements. Listing these elements in an entry of October 27, he felt confident enough to say, "This is what makes November" (*J,* 11:254). A sentence like this illustrates the degree to which November as a calendrical unit has been replaced by November as an aesthetic, phenomenological category of thought. What "makes" November is not its placement in the year's chronology, but its interrelated properties. The very fact that it is "made," constituted, emphasizes the creative role of the perceiver and the categorical imagination.

That this particular observation was made in late October merely confirms that "November" is a category only tangentially related to the calendar month of November. As early as October 8, Thoreau had begun to anticipate its manifestations: "the shore begins to look Novemberish." On November 9, he described "a true November sunset" and observed that some oaks had "assumed their true November aspect." And on November 10, he identified "the silvery light reflected from a myriad of downy surfaces" as "a November phenomenon." But these manifestations of "November" need not have appeared in its calendar month. This is merely the time when they are most likely to appear.

On December 12, for example, Thoreau noted of a Concord landscape that "November lingers still there" (*J,* 11 : 202, 304, 302, 307, 371).

When we turn to Thoreau's Kalendar, we find, along with the charts for April, May, June, and November, an extensive list of natural phenomena for October. The items on this list were almost certainly to have been the phenomenological categories for a chart, suggesting strongly that Thoreau was preparing to schematize October as well. Assuming that the Kalendar is incomplete, and that, had he lived longer, Thoreau would have drawn up charts for other months, we can speculate that November was completed and that October was imminent because these were the fall months whose phenomena had crystallized for him. And while he did not live to chart October, his late essay, "Autumnal Tints," characterizes this month in richly phenomenological terms (*W,* 5 : 249–89). Executed in a different mode, this essay is undoubtedly part of the same conceptual endeavor as Thoreau's chart of November, and these two documents can stand as counterparts. Both emerge out of a long process of category-formation.

But the Kalendar may not be so incomplete as it seems. Perhaps Thoreau charted only those months that had fully transcended their calendrical status for him, that could themselves be considered "seasons." We know, for example, that "[t]he three spring months, and also October and November" were of particular interest to Thoreau because they were "transition months" (March 23, 1860: *J,* 13 : 212), months especially worthy of his study because of what they could teach him about the nature of change. Perhaps their very changefulness prompted him to search out what in them was permanent and to fix their permanent aspects in spatial form.*

---

*All observations about the status of these charts, including their relative completeness, must remain speculative until further evidence about them surfaces. Lists of natural phenomena for months other than April, May, June, October, and November exist in various holdings. For example, the Henry E. Huntington Library and Art Gallery in San Marino, California, has a list of January phenomena (HM 954), and the Berg Collection of the New York Public Library has fragments of a list for February. For a catalogue of these and other, similar manuscript materials, see William L. Howarth, *The Literary Manuscripts of Henry David Thoreau* (Columbus: Ohio State University Press, 1974), 306–31.

That Thoreau's desire to apprehend the seasons spatially, categorically, rather than as a drifting continuum of change, has psychological roots, is suggested by the following Journal passage from December 5, 1856: "I love the winter, with its imprisonment and its cold, for it compels the prisoner to try new fields and resources. I love to have the river closed up for a season and a pause put to my boating. . . . I love best to have each thing in its season only, and enjoy doing without it at all other times" (*J,* 9:160).[9] Thoreau wished to answer in the affirmative, as often as possible, the question he asks regarding the quality of twilight reflections in Walden Pond during the winter of 1853: "Is this phenomenon peculiar to this season[?]" (December 8, 1853: *J,* 6:14).

To "have each thing in its season only" is to achieve an absolute sense of timeliness, to be able to say with confidence (as Thoreau did of the advent of the wild-apple season in 1855), "now is the time" (October 20, 1855: *J,* 7:501). The vision of Thoreau's categorical imagination is that of *Ecclesiastes:*

> There is a season for everything, and we do not notice a given phenomenon except at that season, if, indeed, it can be called the same phenomenon at any other season. There is a time to watch the ripples on Ripple Lake, to look for arrowheads, to study the rocks and lichens, a time to walk on sandy deserts; and the observer of nature must improve these seasons as much as the farmer his. [April 24, 1859: *J,* 12:159]

To "improve these seasons as much as the farmer his" is to cultivate them richly through perception and to fix them in enduring phenomenological categories.

One of the most obvious signs of Thoreau's ongoing revision of the traditional calendar in the Journal is his unceasing recording of first-observed appearances of seasonal phenomena. These observations cluster in the spring, when their myriad occurrences signify the vigorous rebirth of nature celebrated in the climactic chapter of *Walden.* Yet a close reading of the Journal reveals that Thoreau was closely attentive to "first facts" at all seasons.[10] There are hundreds of such observations in the Journal, recorded at all times of the year and usually without commentary. In part, they are an expression of Thoreau's deep preoccupation with origins. By searching the world for the first visible appearances of natural growth, he hopes to participate through observation in the creativity of nature—to be there at the moment of genesis. A passage from a Journal entry of June 2, 1854, expresses this desire poignantly: "I would fain be present at the birth of shadow. It takes place with the first expansion of the leaves" (*J*, 6:323).

But as this example shows, the concept of beginning as it is usually expressed in the Journal is defined not by pure origination but by repetition. The necessary context for observing the "first" appearance of a seasonal phenomenon is the natural cycle; any "first" in nature is recognizable only because it has happened before. That is, Thoreau has already prepared, or recognized, a category for anticipating it; he is keyed for the observation of first facts. In the spring of 1860, we find him "on the alert for several days to hear the first birds" (March 9, 1860: *J*, 13:188). Reporting the appearance of these "first birds" to his Journal is an act of confirmation as much as an act of origination; the beginning, in Thoreau, always pivots between memory and anticipation. As he puts it in a Journal entry of June 6, 1857, "Each annual phenomenon is a reminiscence and prompting" (*J*, 9:406–7).

But even the most vigilant of nature's observers cannot "be present at the birth of shadow," and Thoreau is acutely aware of this, as he shows in an entry of March 17, 1857: "No mortal is alert enough to be present at the first dawn of the spring" (*J*, 9:295). The limitations of individual observation are evident in many places in the Journal, as in an entry of April 8, 1854: "I am surprised to find Walden completely open. When did it open?" (*J*, 6:191). The question "How long?", which becomes a virtual refrain in the late Journal, always sounds slightly plaintive because it signals Thoreau's awareness that he has missed the initial appearance of a phenomenon and therefore has lost *this* year's opportunity to mark its onset.[11]

Yet "How long?" not only laments a lost opportunity; it also implicitly estimates a phenomenon's duration since its unobserved beginning; it is guesswork. And guesswork is a vital part of measuring the seasons and marking their transitions: "It [sweet-gale] is abundantly out at Pinxter Swamp, and has been some time; so I think I may say that the very first opened April 1st" (April 13, 1860: *J,* 13 : 245). By witnessing or closely approximating all of a season's first phenomena, Thoreau would be able to draw the forward edge of that season with a clear, hard line. To mark the beginning so decisively and comprehensively would be to strike the chimes of nature's clock and to hear the music of the spheres.[12] The language of *Walden* comes to mind: "To anticipate, not the sunrise and the dawn merely, but, if possible, Nature herself!" (17).

Everything I am writing about beginnings in the Journal can also be applied to endings. Although Thoreau noted them less frequently, he was as interested in a season's final manifestations as he was in those marking its initiation, and recorded them as carefully: "I think I heard the last lesser redpolls near the beginning of this month; say about 7th" (March 26, 1860: *J,* 13 : 229); "This is about the last of the very dry leaves" (May 6, 1859: *J,* 12 : 184); "The vernal freshness of June is passed" (July 12, 1860: *J,* 13 : 399). He was especially interested in dramatic endings, because they drew seasonal boundaries so emphatically: "It is a great change produced in one frosty night. What a sudden period put to the reign of summer!" (September 9, 1857: *J,* 10 : 29). And late in his life, especially during the fall of 1859, he became acutely interested in what he called the "prime" or "height" of a season's phenomena. On October 14, 1859, for example, he compiled a list of plants and trees "in their mellow prime" (*J,* 12 : 383), as a way of calculating the apex of autumn. To delineate a season's beginning, middle, and end phenomenologically was, for Thoreau, to gather its essential features into a well-defined frame of perception.

Thoreau's methodical and persistent visual circumscription of the seasons reminds us of his work as a surveyor, to which it bears a close spiritual affinity. On December 31, 1857, he reports to his Journal a recent conversation with a neighbor whose property he had been surveying: "He said he didn't want to make bounds, and asked me if I should have set [a boundary stake] there, to which I answered, 'Yes, of course,' that was what I had been doing all my life, making bounds, or rather finding them, remaking what had been unmade, where they were away" (*J,* 10 : 232). As calendar-maker and surveyor, Thoreau is walking through the world to restore the ancient boundaries of time and space. The larger goal toward which this ambulation works is the restoration of the unity of self and world, and this is the ultimate purpose of Thoreau's calendar.

When completed, this calendar would tell us not only of spring's return, which the traditional calendar indicates in any case, but of spring's vivid material presence—its variety and particularity. In reminding us of spring, it actually helps to bring spring into being. This is part of what Thoreau means when he asks in his Journal, on April 18, 1852, "Can I not by expectation affect the revolutions of nature—make a day to bring forth something new?" (*J*, 3:438). Following a phenomenological calendar reinserts the human presence into nature and ignites the creative process of "correspondence." The calendar-maker is doing the work, profoundly ameliorative, of Emerson's "poet."

Furthermore, observing change through the prism of a phenomenological calendar lifts us from the linear and destructive time of history dramatized in *A Week* and embedded in the almanacs of New England. Such historical time is running too fast and is thus running down, exhausting itself. We need a calendar that can teach us the lesson of the turtle: "Be not in haste; mind your private affairs. Consider the turtle. . . . Perchance you have worried yourself, despaired of the world, meditated the end of life, and all things seemed rushing to destruction; but nature has steadily and serenely advanced with a turtle's pace. . . . Has not the tortoise . . . learned the true value of time?" (August 28, 1856: *J*, 9:32–33).

The cricket, too, has "learned the true value of time":

> The song of [a cricket] . . . suggests lateness, but only as we come to a knowledge of eternity after some acquaintance with time. It is only late for all trivial and hurried pursuits. It suggests a wisdom mature, never late, being above all temporal considerations. . . . So they chant, eternal, at the roots of the grass. . . . A quire [of crickets] knows only the eternal. [May 22, 1854: *J*, 6:290–91]

The "Sounds" chapter of *Walden* is, perhaps, Thoreau's most eloquent evocation of this vision of the eternal. But his most important instrument for gaining "some acquaintance with time" and thus coming into "a knowledge of eternity" is the Journal, whose procedure is summed up in the following passage of April 7, 1853: "If you make the least correct observation of nature this year—you will have occasion to repeat it with illustrations the next, and the season & life itself is prolonged" (*J*, 5:100). Such prolongation is the result of learning nature's long, slow, "unhurried" rhythms.

Thoreau's phenomenological calendar, we may say, is addressed to the same people to whom *Walden* is addressed, those so distracted by civilization that they have lost contact with nature: "Every year men talk about the dry weather which has now begun as if it were something new and not to be expected" (June 18, 1854: *J*, 6:370). As the judgmental quality of this remark suggests, the inability to anticipate the particular manifestations of a season is, in part, a perceptual (and thus moral) failing. Yet Thoreau is aware of a larger, innate human failing: the full annual cycle is a unit of time too great for most people's capacity to hold specific developments vividly in memory. As Thoreau writes in a Journal entry of March 18, 1858, "Each new year is a surprise to us. We find that we had virtually forgotten the note of each bird, and when we hear it again it is remembered like a dream, reminding us of a previous state of existence" (*J*, 10:304).

That this failure belongs specifically to Thoreau, as well as to the rest of us, is suggested by the way he experienced the beginning of winter in 1856: "It seemed as if winter had come without any interval since midsummer, and I was prepared to see it flit away by the time I again looked over my shoulder. It was as if I had dreamed it" (December 7, 1856: *J*, 9:168). To restore the "interval," the demarcation that "truly" marks the distinctive and vivid properties of seasonal change, is to be re-minded, made mindful, of nature itself and awakened from our dream. This is morning work.

At issue, then, is the way in which human beings necessarily experience duration:

> Each season is but an infinitesimal point. It no sooner comes than it is gone. It has no duration. . . . Our thoughts and sentiments answer to the revolutions of the seasons, as two cog-

wheels fit into each other. We are conversant with only one point
of contact at a time, from which we receive a prompting and impulse and instantly pass to a new season or point of contact.
[June 6, 1857: *J*, 9:406–7]

The purpose of a phenomenological calendar is to overcome this limitation by organizing the myriad "point[s] of contact" (perceptions) into a
coherent vision, and thus to teach us an "acquaintance with time."
But, in its very nature, such cumulative knowledge comes slowly:
"Young men have not learned the phases of Nature; they do not know
what constitutes a year, or that one year is like another" (September 24,
1859: *J*, 12:347). "It takes us many years," Thoreau writes on May 5,
1860, "to find out that Nature repeats herself annually. But how per-
fectly regular and calculable all her phenomena must appear to a mind
that has observed her for a thousand years!" (*J*, 13:279). This "mind"
is the temporal perspective toward which Thoreau's Journal unceas-
ingly strives. Gaining even a small portion of its view would make one
"an assured inhabitant of the earth" (December 19, 1859: *J*, 13:35).

THE ROUGH AND THE SMOOTH: FILLING THE CATEGORIES

From a late-twentieth-century perspective, Thoreau's effort to make a
"truer" calendar is filled with difficulty, in part because our notion of
truth itself has changed so radically since his day. We may take as a
key example Thoreau's work as a surveyor of time, seeking out the
"true" beginnings and endings of seasons. As Edward Said and Frank
Kermode have reminded us in different contexts, beginnings and endings are always fictional, always impossible to isolate and mark without
uncovering some other beginning or ending whose claim to authenticity is equally valid.[13] And, it may be added, the "middle" or "prime"
is just as fictional a moment within the flux of duration.

Even allowing for the possibility of a "true" beginning, how is it
possible to know that one has perceived it and not something ficti-
tious? That Thoreau was at least peripherally aware of the latter problem is evident from the emphasis he often gives to verbs of perception,
as in the following passage from July 22, 1854: "First *noticed* the dry

scent of corn-fields a week ago" (*J,* 6:407). Sentences like these, of which there are many in the Journal, share the sense of uncertainty and regret expressed in Thoreau's often-repeated question "How long?" But, as we have seen, such uncertainty was largely resolved to Thoreau's satisfaction by the Journal itself: in its capacity to "remember" the initial, perceived moment of each year's seasonal phenomena, it would slowly, incrementally, take him from approximation to certainty.

The difficulties of Thoreau's calendar-making for the modern reader often show up as inconsistencies and anomalies. Sometimes, for example, nature would seem to mark its beginnings and endings with such clarity that they could not be missed—revealing the structure of seasonal change like the hands of a clock: "It is the 3 o'clock P.M. of the year when they [yellow flowers] begin to prevail" (August 12, 1854: *J,* 6:433). At such times the "true" transitions between seasons are unmistakable: "it [the leafing of birches] marks an epoch in the season, the *transition* decidedly and generally from bare twigs to leaves" (May 17, 1854: *J,* 6:275; Thoreau's emphasis). Then Thoreau could actually experience the "crossing [of] the threshold between winter and summer" and vividly "realize that a new season has arrived" (March 30, 1860: *J,* 13:235). On August 4, 1856, for example, he knew, from the sound of "the alder *cricket,*" that "[t]he turning point [from summer to autumn] is reached" (*J,* 8:444). The Journal is filled, during the 1850s and the early 1860s, with confident pronouncements such as these from 1852: "Now is the summer come"; "Now it is true autumn" (May 30 and October 11, 1852: *J,* 4:75, 382).

Yet there were other times when he was far less sure of seasonal boundaries, when nature's transitions would slip by unobserved. The summer of 1854 was such a time: "The spring now seems far behind, yet I do not remember the interval. I feel as if some broad invisible lethean gulf lay behind, between this and spring" (July 2, 1854: *J,* 6:382). Later that month, Thoreau wrote in his Journal a sentence whose interrupted syntax betrays the difficulty: "We seem to be passing, or to have passed, a dividing line between spring and autumn, and begin to descend the long slope toward winter" (July 15, 1854: *J,* 6:395).

In part, this difficulty stems from a question of deep perplexity to the nineteenth-century romantic mind: to what degree was the apprehension of truth an objective or subjective process? Like Emerson, Thoreau was committed to a perspectival search for truth. "Your observation, to be interesting, *i.e.* to be significant," he wrote in an entry of May 6, 1854, "must be *subjective*" (*J*, 6:237; Thoreau's emphasis). And this applied, at least some of the time, to his apprehension of seasonal change. The following question, from a Journal entry of the same month, seems to assert rhetorically that the standard for judging the summer's beginning is altogether private: "Is not this the first day of summer, when first I sit with the window open and forget fire?" (May 11, 1854: *J*, 6:261). Yet only a month later Thoreau speculated about summer's onset in different terms: "The summer aspect of the river begins perhaps when the *Utricularia vulgaris* is first seen on the surface, as yesterday" (June 9, 1854: *J*, 6:336). Here perception remains central, but the tentativeness of the expression ("perhaps"), as well as its passive construction ("is first seen"), suggest a public, almost empirical standard against which private, subjective experience must be measured. Thoreau's Journal, throughout, exhibits a richly inconsistent mixture of objective and subjective visions of nature.*

But the essential problem of Thoreau's calendar-making was his determination to conceive of time phenomenologically. On the one hand, this strategy liberated him from the tyranny of chronological time and brought him into an intimate relation with nature as it manifested itself through change—as in, for example, the flow of earth from the railroad cut depicted in *Walden*. But to actually structure time phenomenologically, to construct a calendar from phenomena, started a process that could not be ended, even as the idea of a calendar (a schematization of time) insisted on closure. As long as visual (or, more broadly, sensory) integrity was the standard for marking time, then seasonal categories would always be giving way to other, more integral categories—categories "truer" to perception.

Complicating the matter further is that any newly emergent seasonal

---

*This mixture is reflected in the categories Thoreau developed for his Kalendar. See the Appendix for a discussion of this aspect of the Kalendar.

category could be shaken, at any time, by an observation that didn't fit. There are many instances in the Journal of Thoreau's perplexity upon discovering such anomalies: "This ["red capsules of the *Hypericum ellipticum*"] one of the fallward phenomena in still rainy [summer] days" (July 14, 1854: *J*, 6:394). The very act of re-making seasonal boundaries and thus demarcating new categories introduced a new level of abstraction that was itself open to challenge. Unmistakably, the seasons—even those, such as "the reign of water," recognized and named by Thoreau himself—were always drifting one into the next, and at every turn categories were sliding out of focus. His response to this, as I have said, was not to relinquish his categories but to make them ever more precise.

But the problem with making temporal categories ever more precise is that of Zeno's paradox. In a continuum of change, where can lines of division be drawn authentically? Is not any line fundamentally arbitrary? Where, "truly," do seasonal boundaries lie, and what is the nature of such truth? For every gradient of change there is still another, smaller gradient whose phenomena might more vividly characterize the temporal moment. Thoreau intended the following sentence from a Journal entry of September 10, 1860, as a celebration of nature's diversity, but it also identifies his fundamental difficulty: "Almost every plant, however humble, has thus its day, and sooner or later becomes the characteristic feature of some part of the landscape or other" (*J*, 14:77).

Ordering time phenomenologically inevitably led Thoreau to subdivide the seasons; by the mid-1850s we find him systematically searching the world for "early spring phenomen[a]" and for "*late* phenomena of spring" (March 3, 1855: *J*, 7:229; May 21, 1854: *J*, 6:284). Ultimately, each of the four traditional seasons was subdivided in this way, as well as in many others even more purely phenomenological: "The brightening of the willows or of osiers,—that is a season in the spring" (February 24, 1855: *J*, 7:212). Potentially, the process was endless; it could lead to seasonal subdivisions as small as a single day: "This [gossamer], then, is a phenomenon of the first warm and calm day after the ground is bare" (March 16, 1860: *J*, 13:197–98).

If Thoreau's categorical imagination began its work by expanding categories from those denoting and highlighting the features of a single day to those that embraced larger spans of time, by the late 1850s it was focusing on ever more delimited categories. In other words, the late Journal shows Thoreau moving dangerously close to the "maze of phenomena" from which his categorical imagination, at an earlier stage, had served to liberate him. That he ultimately did not enter the maze, or entered it only occasionally, can be attributed to the fact that, in the end, he remained faithful to the basic structure of calendrical time. Spring, summer, fall, and winter—the essential units spanning the circle of time—always loomed in the background as the overarching structure of his thought. This cycle also is the supporting structure of *Walden,* whose dense intertextuality is grounded in and clarified by the progression of the seasons.

The difficulties of Thoreau's calendar-making I have sketched above belong centrally to the romantic age in which he lived. But they inhere in the oldest and most persistent of philosophical questions: What is the nature of change? In a world of flux, what can be called permanent? And since everything we know is known perspectively, subjectively, what claims can the objective, empirical world of things make upon us? The impressive thing about Thoreau's attempt to answer these questions—and this is what the Journal, at large, is implicitly doing all the time—is the degree to which it adumbrates the modern position. In the early twentieth century, Alfred North Whitehead precisely stated this position:

> One all-pervasive fact, inherent in the very character of what is real is the transition of things, the passage one to another. This passage is not a mere linear procession of discrete entities. However we fix a determinate entity, there is always a narrower determination of something which is presupposed in our first choice. Also there is always a wider determination into which our first choice fades by transition beyond itself. The general aspect of nature is that of evolutionary expansiveness. These unities, which I call events, are the emergence into actuality of something. How are we to characterize the something which thus emerges? The

name "*event*" given to such a unity, draws attention to the inherent transitoriness, combined with the actual unity.[14]

Thoreau was unprepared to recognize, and therefore confront, the issue of change explicitly in these terms. Yet his Journal, in procedure if not in conceptualization, anticipates to a remarkable degree the solution that Whitehead offers to the modern world. Whitehead's "event," which he calls a "grasping into unity of a pattern of aspects,"[15] serves the same purpose as Thoreau's category: to validate the emergence of "things" into unity and coherence in a world constantly changing before our eyes. Like Whitehead's event, Thoreau's category is a perceptual construct that exists in and of the world, and in this sense dramatizes the relation between self and world.

Thoreau thus points toward twentieth-century thought without quite arriving at the modern position; his Journal is an intriguingly proto-modern document. Given a fuller recognition of what his procedures implied, Thoreau might have found his way to the pragmatic, instrumental vision of truth espoused by Whitehead and John Dewey. But this step would have required that he relinquish his great nineteenth-century, romantic dream: "I wish to know an entire heaven and an entire earth" (March 23, 1856: *J*, 8:221). And, ironically, the Journal's provisional, open form—itself so strikingly modern—confirmed for Thoreau the possibility of gaining such knowledge. The Journal promised him that every season, repeated in the annual round, would offer new opportunities to draw the design of nature in its grand totality. In always presenting another page to fill, it fed his desire for a fully comprehensive vision of the natural and supernatural worlds.

In other words, the method of the Journal was not the open-ended, pragmatic test of truth that its form suggests to us. Instead, the test of the Journal's efficacy for Thoreau was the fullness of its vision, and its method was to fill its emergent categories to repletion. Of all natural phenomena, he wished to be able to say, as he did of a scene he was observing on May 19, 1854: "I have already described the oaks sufficiently" (*J*, 6:280). This sufficiency of vision is closely related to the "ripeness" celebrated in *Walden,* and *Walden* itself may be understood as a heavily elaborated category of perception, a frame of refer-

ence, continuous with Journal categories such as "the reign of water"
and "November."

In strictly chronological terms, *Walden* abbreviates experience, con-
densing two years into one. But in phenomenological terms it enlarges
experience, filling up, through imaginative association, the perceptual
category known as "Walden" with as many interrelated phenomena as
possible. *Walden,* as a "little world" with a vast network of "likeness,"
is a realization of the aesthetic ideal that Thoreau found reflected in
"the colors of the withered oak leaves": "We want the greatest variety
within the smallest compass, and yet without glaring diversity" (December 4, 1856: *J,* 9:153).

As with so many other aspects of the Journal's development, the desire for comprehensiveness becomes part of a conscious agenda in the
early 1850s. We can see it formally stated as an objective in a passage of
November 10, 1851, where Thoreau calls for a "true and absolute account of things—of the evening & the morning & all the phenomena
between them" (*J,* 3:103–4). The Kalendar is the most literal expression of this intent, as well as (from our point of view) the most vivid
testimony to the impossibility of its fulfillment. Many of the spaces in
the charts are empty. But these empty spaces, clearly inviting inscription and thereby assuming the possibility of repleteness, are filled with
Thoreau's desire.

In the Kalendar, repleteness has been abstracted into a set of paradigms, whereas in *Walden* it has to some extent become a principle of
life, "ripeness," part of the agenda of self-reform. For the most spontaneous expression of Thoreau's desire for repleteness, we must turn
to the Journal, where it often appears in marginal situations such as
afterthoughts. An entry of March 7, 1854, begins: "I did not mention
the drifts yesterday" (*J,* 6:155). Often, recalling a list of natural phenomena he had compiled earlier, Thoreau will become mindful of an
omission. On July 18, 1851, for example, he writes, "I might have
added to the list of July 16th The Aralia hispida Bristling aralia— The
heart-leaved Loosestrife Lysimachia ciliata— [etc.]" (*PJ,* 3:313). And,
following a list made in an entry of May 27, 1854, he writes, "To this
add the hum and creak of insects" (*J,* 6:307). In all such cases we
sense the writer making sure that not a single thing has been omitted.

Lists very much like the ones referred to above became the basis for constructing Thoreau's Kalendar. They were the intermediate step between his firsthand observations, as recorded in his Journal, and the formation of the Kalendar's categories. But these lists, as well as those in the Journal, have a life and identity of their own. The very act of "listing," of setting down a long series of things that go together, betray a mind bent upon getting everything down. No less than Whitman's catalogues, to which they bear a close formal and spiritual affinity, Thoreau's lists (and the activity of listing) strive toward the fullest possible vision of life.

These lists, of course, are also part of Thoreau's work as a naturalist, of his pursuit of scientific data, comprehensively and accurately described, through classification. Yet, again, this pursuit must be understood within the larger framework of his desire for repleteness. And this desire is characteristic not only of Thoreau's lists, but of the Journal as a whole. This is a document whose ultimate goal is indeed a "true and absolute account of things." But a mind given to a full, exhaustive tally of experience needs limits; otherwise, the sheer volume and variety of observation may overwhelm perception. There is a fine line between completeness and chaos, between filling categories and allowing them to overflow. This observation brings us back to the categorical imagination and its possible psychological sources in Thoreau. That it has deep psychic roots is suggested by a dream from childhood that he recounts in a Journal entry of January 7, 1857:

> *There,* in that Well Meadow Field, perhaps, I feel in my element again, as when a fish is put back into the water. I wash off all my chagrins. All things go *smoothly* as the *axle of the universe.* I can remember that when I was very young I used to have a dream night after night, over and over again, which might have been named Rough and Smooth. All existence, all satisfaction and dissatisfaction, all event was symbolized in this way. Now I seemed to be lying and tossing, perchance, on a horrible, a fatal rough surface, which must soon, indeed, put an end to my existence, though even in the dream I knew it to be the symbol merely of my misery; and then again, suddenly, I was lying on a delicious

smooth surface, as of a summer sea, as of gossamer or down or softest plush, and life was such a luxury to live. My waking experience *always* has been and is such an alternate Rough and Smooth. In other words it is Insanity and Sanity. [*J,* 9 : 210–11; emphases added in third sentence]

We should first notice the sentence, "All things go smoothly as the axle of the universe." Apparently unrelated (though immediately prior) to the description of the dream's dramatic polarity, it nevertheless anticipates the most fundamental definition of the smooth. The smooth, for Thoreau, is intimately associated with the circle of time ("the axle of the universe"), whose essential values are coherence, order, and predictability. The circle of time was for him the image that quieted chaos and restored order.

Thoreau's terms for his dream's polar experiences, rough and smooth, are, of course, retrospectively assigned; the dream itself did not name them so. Yet this naming, while retrospective, is not so arbitrary as Thoreau's phrasing ("[they] might have been named Rough and Smooth") would suggest. The terms have their home in Burkean landscape aesthetics, and while Thoreau doesn't mention this derivation, it would not have been possible for him to ignore their pictorial meanings.[16] When he wrote this passage, Thoreau had already studied Gilpin with care and was about to take up Ruskin in earnest. Thoreau's use of these terms in describing his dream makes it clear that his own aesthetic of nature—his picture of the world—was grounded deeply in psychological imperatives. Rough and smooth, chaos and cosmos, relation and category—these are the ruling terms of Thoreau's imaginative life, and at every stage they inform his aesthetic of nature.

In making this statement, we must remind ourselves that whatever Thoreau absorbed from Gilpin and Ruskin about landscape views, his aesthetic of nature has deeper sources. As we saw, its basic design is already well formed by the time he came to Gilpin in the spring of 1852, and his recounting of this dream suggests that throughout the decade of the 1850s he was coming into contact with his own deepest spatial imagination—the contours of the self—which found expression in his greatest literary achievement of this period, *Walden.*

The "summer sea" of the passage, an image cognate with Walden Pond, suggests maternal repose, the "structure" of the womb. Similarly, "gossamer" (a natural phenomenon noted repeatedly in the Journal) is an image of softly reticulated form, but its delicacy and vulnerability imply how easily the smooth becomes rough (or "ruffled," to borrow from the language of *Walden*), how easily the rough asserts itself, making chaos of cosmos. In the terms of our present discussion, the rough is the "wild," creative ego that seeks relation, whereas the smooth is the shaping category in which such activity is safely contained.

And this polarity, in turn, must be seen as an aspect of a still larger psychological polarity between differentiation and unity, between the roughness of the "Many" and the smoothness of the "One."[17] Thoreau's equation of roughness with insanity suggests his view of the human being in society—the adult, social realm of individuated selves—which, as he characterizes it in *Walden,* is indeed insane, even if its desperation is quiet. The "One"—a union of the childhood self with nature—is the fundamental structure that Thoreau is always seeking, and Walden Pond is the "landscape of [his] infant dreams" (156) in this particular sense.

From another perspective, the rough is analogous to the experience of radical defamiliarization that Thoreau experienced on Mount Katahdin and at Cape Cod, whereas the smooth corresponds to the total familiarization of landscape that the writer achieved at Walden.[18] The Pond itself, of course, is the most poignant image of the smooth in all of Thoreau's writings. As a perceptual category, the Walden experience (and the book called *Walden*) is a perfect "container" of the Rough. It is a "pastoral" exactly according to the definition that William Empson long ago gave this genre: it contains the tensions it exhibits, and in this way recalls certain other great American literary landscapes, such as James Fenimore Cooper's Glimmerglass in *The Deerslayer.*[19]

When the shoreline of Walden is viewed as the boundary of a perceptual category, it shakes off some of the symbolism of an encroaching civilization that critics have traditionally assigned to it.[20] Instead, the shoreline becomes the design, the categorical framework, in which Walden's variegated, flowing currents of diverse meaning and association are contained and understood; it gives shape to the experience that *Walden* describes. And if, from another point of view, Walden's currents and eddies, its ripples and ruffles, symbolize the flow of time (like the rivers of *A Week*), then its shoreline can be considered the spatial context in which those currents are held in check.

Thoreau's careful measurement of the Pond is itself a structuring, a confirming of its boundaries and the perfect symmetry that they create. This process of measurement is analogous to the technique of the artist Fitz Hugh Lane, whose landscape *Norman's Woe* (1862) was painted from a precisely drawn grid.[21] Both this painting and *Walden* create the effect of mobile equilibrium. They stand poised in a kind of permanence, even as we sense their potential for reconfiguration. One can always imagine another Walden, another perceptual category called Walden, contoured differently, more capaciously, standing just beyond it. This is one of the meanings of the famous phrase near the narrative's close: "I had several more lives to live" (323).

In other words, Walden Pond is drawn in a form exactly analogous to the circle of time, the "axle of the universe," and as a work of art is the most profound expression of Thoreau's discovery of this design.

Fitz Hugh Lane, *Norman's Woe,* 1862. Cape Ann Historical Association, Gloucester, Massachusetts.

Herbert W. Gleason, *South Shore of Walden Pond, Reflections of Trees, from Railroad; May 30, 1903.* The Herbert W. Gleason Collection.

That Thoreau produced the final thrust of creative energy needed to complete *Walden* in the period immediately following his discovery of the circle is more than coincidental.[22]

April 18, 1852, is the day on which Thoreau declared his first apprehension of the circle of time. Immediately following this declaration, in a paragraph belonging to the same Journal entry, he continued his thoughts in this way:

> Why should just these sights & sounds accompany our life? Why should I hear the chattering of blackbirds—why smell the skunk each year? I would fain explore the mysterious relation between myself and these things. I would at least know what these things unavoidably are—make a chart of our life—know how its shores

> trend—that butterflies reappear & when—know why just this
> circle of creatures completes the world. [*J,* 3 : 438]

Thoreau's apprehension of the circle of time prompted these questions, because it validated their premise: that the "circle of creatures
[that] completes the world" was in fact complete. It drew the framework in which the answers to these questions were implicitly anticipated and the process of their being answered was authenticated.
Looking back at this passage from the perspective of the Journal's full
development through 1861, we can see that one answer to this set of
questions was the "chart of our life" that Thoreau drew up in his final
years; his Kalendar was an outgrowth of the empirical observations
made and recorded in his Journal throughout the 1850s. But another,
more "poetic" answer was already partially formulated and only two
years from being rendered. As Thoreau considered why the world is
"worlded" as it is, and why that world so completely fills the arc of our
perception, the answer that came to him was *Walden.*

PART 3
WALDEN

≈≈≈

Finally, the world itself, which . . . is the totality of perceptible things and the thing of all things, must be understood not as an object in the sense the mathematician or the physicist give to this word—that is, a kind of unified law which would cover all the partial phenomena or as a fundamental relation verifiable in all—but as the universal style of all possible perceptions.

—Maurice Merleau-Ponty, "The Primacy of Perception and Its Philosophical Consequences"

five

〰〰〰〰〰〰
〰〰〰〰〰〰

THE
WORLDING
OF WALDEN

W hy do precisely these objects which we behold make a world?" Thoreau asks in "Brute Neighbors," chapter 12 of *Walden.* This is the central question that *Walden* seeks to answer and to which *Walden* itself is an answer. The word "precisely" reveals the assumption underlying the question, with its clear implication that the world as we know it corresponds exactly to our needs and expectations. "Why has man," Thoreau continues, "*just* these species of animals for his neighbors; as if nothing but a mouse could have filled this crevice?" (225; emphasis added). The world we know through perception is a "fitting" world, a world of balance and symmetry. In the terms of our discussion of the Journal, it is a category filled to its exact limits and no more, "a world with full and fair proportions" (327), as Thoreau calls the staff made by the artist of Kouroo.

The brief descriptions of Thoreau's "brute neighbors" that follow these questions are, he seems to say, as full an answer as anyone will ever need: the "mice which haunted my house"; the phoebe that "built in my shed"; the robin that found protection in the pine next to the hut; the partridge that led her brood past the windows; the otter and raccoon that lived nearby; the woodcock probing for worms; the turtledoves that sat over the spring; the red squirrel "coursing down the nearest bough" (225–28).

The simple, enumerative quality of this passage (it resembles both in form and intention one of the Journal's lists) makes clear that these "neighbors" are constituents of a world already organized and prepared by nature for human perception, and that perception, in fact, has very little work to do: "You only need sit still long enough in some attractive spot in the woods that *all* its inhabitants may exhibit themselves to you by turns" (228; emphasis added). Walden is that axial point from which, by simply watching and waiting, one may "behold" the full kaleidoscope of nature's phenomena.

This is the centralized perspective that was announced earlier in the chapter "Where I Lived, and What I Lived For": "Wherever I sat, there I might live, and the landscape radiated from me accordingly" (81). Everything that enters this radius, by definition, belongs to a proximate world, a world of "the nearest bough." Like the red squirrel, all the creatures perceived from this perspective are "familiar" (228) to Thoreau; they are already familiarized, prepared for the imagination by their placement within the world of Walden.

But immediately following this brisk enumeration of the animals and birds in Thoreau's peaceable kingdom, the chapter takes an abrupt turn: "I was witness to events of a less peaceful character" (228). And, indeed, the description of the ant-war that follows shows us a rapacious natural world sharply at odds with that of the turtledove and the phoebe. But what it also shows us is a different mode of apprehension, a different way of "beholding." So often discussed is this famous set piece that I need not recount here the pitched battle of the ants or the brilliant play of metaphor with which it is narrated. For the purpose of this discussion, the most important element of the piece is a Thoreauvian gesture having nothing to do with the battle as such: "I took up the chip on which the three [ants] I have particularly described were struggling, carried it into my house, and placed it under a tumbler on my window-sill, in order to see the issue. Holding a microscope to the first-mentioned red ant, I saw that, though he was assiduously gnawing at the near fore-leg of his enemy . . . his own breast was all torn away" (230–31).

Mere watchful waiting is insufficient to view these brute neighbors (the oxymoron making itself felt in this context). Their size, as well as the complexity of their movements, requires that they be scrutinized under a microscope. For all the self-conscious literary allusiveness of the piece, its dominant spirit is that of the observer-scientist, and the microscope itself is a figure for this analytical mode of apprehension. The naturalist's view of nature makes itself felt often in the Journal, but in *Walden* it is generally subordinated to other, more "aesthetic" modes of apprehension. This is one reason, apart from its hyperbolic and burnished prose, why the ant-war passage sometimes seems out of place, rather like some of the more intrusive digressions in *A Week*.

As different as the ant-war is from the scene that precedes it, however, these passages share one important trait: both the simple beholding of the one and the intense scrutiny of the other are the acts of a subject-viewer totally in control of his perceptions. But now, following Thoreau's description of the ant-war, we find ourselves in the realm of the fortuitous: "Once I was surprised to see a cat walking along the stony shore of the pond, for they rarely wander so far from home"; "Once, when berrying, I met with a cat with young kittens in the woods, quite wild, and they all, like their mother, had their backs up and were fiercely spitting at me" (232).

These instances of the unexpected and the "wild" are followed by the description of a mysterious "'winged cat'" (232), whose presence in the town of Lincoln several years before the Walden experiment was reported to Thoreau by Mrs. Gilian Baker, who had taken it in. Everything about this creature is elusive: when Thoreau goes to see it, it has "gone a-hunting in the woods, as was her wont," and he is "not sure whether it was a male or female" (233). This winged cat, never actually observed by Thoreau, finally becomes a local legend: "Some thought it was part flying-squirrel or some other wild animal, which is not impossible, for, according to naturalists, prolific hybrids have been produced by the union of the marten and domestic cat" (233). But, in the end, no naturalist will ever have the opportunity to examine this strange animal, whose hybrid nature symbolizes its essential mystery and unclassifiability.*

The surprising cats described in this passage prepare us for the wildest of Walden's creatures, the loon.[1] Though its appearance is predictable ("the loon . . . came, as usual" [233]), the announcement of its arrival—"his wild laughter"—signals how unpredictable its actions are. Now the "surprise" caused by the cats is replaced by astonishment, wonder, and disorientation. The sense of the fortuitous increases: "As I was paddling along the north shore one very calm October afternoon, . . . suddenly one [loon], sailing out from the shore toward the middle a few rods in front of me, set up his wild laugh and betrayed himself."

The calm is broken and the chase is on, but Thoreau's pursuit is repeatedly interrupted, his expectations defeated at every "turn": "He dived again, but I miscalculated the direction he would take" (234); "again and again, when I was straining my eyes over the surface one way, I would suddenly be startled by his unearthly laugh behind me" (235). The loon's laugh, as well as its "long-drawn unearthly howl" (236), are the sounds of the uncanny: "the wildest sound that is ever heard here" (236). In contrast to the winged cat, here is a creature that never can be domesticated.

The loon's "demoniac laughter" (236) is mocking; unlike the gentle creatures that surround the hut, the loon insists upon its separateness from its observer. Thoreau's failed pursuit of the loon dramatizes this creature's refusal to be contained (familiarized) within the Edenic vision of Walden sketched earlier in the chapter, or to be brought under the naturalist's microscrope, as in the ant-war passage. It exists in a realm beyond the proximate world of Thoreau's hut. (Here is a creature at home in all dimensions, in water and sky, in the depths and heights of Walden.) The entire scene emphasizes the independence of object from subject: "While he was thinking one thing in his brain, I

---

*Thoreau secures a set of the creature's "wings," but he does not report having studied them, and their import in the passage is to intensify rather than diminish the mystery.

was endeavoring to divine his thought in mine." Unlike the ants, which Thoreau picks up and takes indoors to examine, his "adversary" (235) the loon escapes him, "disappearing far away on the tumultuous surface" (236).

But if the loon insists upon its separateness from Thoreau, scenically they are one. Hunter and hunted (it is a visual hunt) merge into a single ambience, a dance between subject and object: "It was a pretty game, played on the smooth surface of the pond, a man against a loon" (235). The "against" of the final phrase may remind us of the antagonism of the ant-war, but surely Thoreau also intends the word in a pictorial sense: a man *set against* the background of a loon and both set against the background of Walden, which is the stage on which their drama unfolds.

To a greater degree than any of the preceding sections of "Brute Neighbors," the loon passage invites us to picture Thoreau himself within the scene, so that the scene—in its totality—becomes the object of the reader's eye. ("[C]an we separate the man," Emerson asks in *Nature,* "from the living picture?" [*CW,* 1 : 15].) Thoreau is too busy pursuing the loon to really behold it; it is we who do the beholding, and as we do so a world comes into being.

The diving and plunging of the loon, as well as Thoreau's pursuit, are part of a lovely dance between the self and nature, in something of the sense that Suzanne Langer intends when she says that "dance creates a world of powers" and shows us "a display of interacting forces."[2] Around these images of power and force, the dance merges with the hunt. Thoreau is a "hunter" of the loon, not in the sense of predation, but in the sense described by José Ortega y Gasset in his *Meditations on Hunting:* "All means of pursuit and capture which the hunter employs correspond to countermeasures of evasion that the prey employs," dramatizing "a relationship in which two systems of instincts confront each other."[3]

Not only is the loon a symbol of Thoreau's own spiritual deep-diving, as most critics have viewed it. It also is a pure dramatization, or "immanence," of the relation between man and loon—a relation founded more on difference than on similarity. Without difference, without otherness, there could be no dance. The relationship that Thoreau describes as "a man against a loon" should thus also be understood as an encounter, in which the loon emerges "over against" the spatial "background" of the Pond. These are the terms Martin Buber employs to describe the encounter between "I" and "Thou," in which the greatest intimacy (in Thoreau's terms, "correspondence") results from the full "emergence" of "Thou." * For Thoreau to "divine [the loon's] thought in mine" is, ultimately, to make this encounter, and, in doing so, to discover the "wildness" that resides within himself.

This great passage, then, introduces still another form of beholding that characterizes *Walden* at some of its most powerful and lyric moments. To behold in this way is to emphasize the "holding," not in the sense of possession, but in the sense of a vibrant, organic world brought into being and "held" steadily before us. Unlike the scene of watchful waiting depicted earlier in "Brute Neighbors," the loon passage emphasizes the self as a creator (a dancer and hunter, in this sense as well) in the world beheld.

This thought returns us, of course, to the artist of Kouroo, whose own "world of full and fair proportions" was "made" in exactly this way: "When the finishing stroke was put to his work, it suddenly *expanded* before the eyes of the *astonished* artist into the fairest of all the creations of Brahma" (327; emphases added). The creation of this staff ("a new system") brings a world into being and sustains it through imagination. We may also be reminded of the mythical creation of Walden itself, "the work of a brave man . . . [who] rounded this water with his hand" (193).

The loon passage implicitly revises Thoreau's earlier answer to the question "Why do precisely these objects which we behold make a world?" The fullest answer to this question is that objects do not, by

*The relevant passage from Buber follows: "The *Thou* appears, to be sure, in space, but in the exclusive situation of what is over against it, where everything else can be only the background out of which it emerges, not its boundary and measured limit" (*I and Thou,* 2d ed., trans. Ronald G. Smith [New York: Charles Scribner's Sons, 1958], 30).

themselves, make a world; worlds are "made" by the interaction—the "dance"—of the creative self and the world. This is the same answer that the Journal, through its continuous play of association, gives over and over again through the long course of its development.

But "Brute Neighbors" concludes with a return to the mode of apprehension with which it began, that of watchful waiting: "For hours, in fall days, I watched the ducks cunningly tack and veer and hold the middle of the pond. . . . When compelled to rise they would sometimes circle round and round and over the pond at a considerable height" (236–37). The ducks' veering and circling suggest the loon's movements, but here the perceiver remains stationary, contemplative, a viewer rather than an actor in the scene. But this final scene is not merely a "frame" for the great loon passage, a way of highlighting its drama. Rather, its placement reminds us that contemplation is, as much as the "dance," a way of involving oneself in nature. Both watchful waiting from a stationary, centralized perspective, as well as the joyful dance of creation, are avenues to "correspondence," and *Walden* is characterized by a movement back and forth between these modes. In this, it closely resembles Whitman's "Song of Myself," which validates both "loafing" and "[s]peeding through space" as means to fulfillment. Like Whitman, Thoreau is "[b]oth in and out of the game" (secs. 1, 5, 33, 4).

Thus, the chapter "Brute Neighbors" may be understood as pivotal; it presents in anecdotal form the two most important modes of apprehension characterizing *Walden* as a whole. On the one hand, its scenes of watchful waiting recall the "serenity" (193) of "The Ponds," where we found Thoreau "floating over [Walden's] surface as the zephyr willed, having paddled my boat to the *middle,* and lying on my back across the seats, in a summer forenoon, dreaming awake" (191; emphasis added). This is the perspective of centralized solitude whose aesthetic and spiritual advantages were asserted earlier in the same chapter: "The forest has never so good a setting, nor is so distinctly beautiful, as when seen from the middle of a small lake" (185).

On the other hand, the loon passage of "Brute Neighbors" anticipates the climactic chapter "Spring," with its dramatization of a flowing, "living" earth and of a beholder intimately involved in nature's processes. In that chapter, Thoreau's "alert[ness] for the first signs of spring" (302), like his anticipation of the loon's initial appearance, signals a participatory role. (As Ortega says, "[t]he hunter is the alert man" whose alertness takes him to "an authentic 'outside,'" to the condition of being "*within* the countryside.")[4] And like the unpredictable loon or the "surprising" cats, the "sand foliage" is remarkable because of "its springing into existence thus *suddenly*" (306; emphasis added). As much as the loon, the sand foliage suggests transformation to Thoreau: "The very globe continually transcends and translates itself, and becomes winged in its orbit" (306–7). Finally, "Spring" follows the loon passage in its rendering of a world "made" through creation and still in the process of being created: "I am affected as if in a peculiar sense I stood in the laboratory of the Artist [the phrase conjoins science and art] who made the world and me,—had come to where he was still at work, sporting on this bank, and with excess of energy strewing his fresh designs about" (306).

But the distinction between the contemplative and creative modes of apprehension, as they are depicted in *Walden,* can be overdrawn. The contemplative mode involves its own form of engagement with the natural world. Reverie, as Bachelard reminds us, is an active process; it is what Whitman called inviting the soul. In his philosophical meditation, *The Inward Morning* (a phrase taken from Thoreau), Henry Bugbee describes this process: "The present in question seems to expand itself extensively into temporal and spatial distances. And it is as if one's perception of everything distinct were engaged in alignment with a center from which one moves to greet each thing knowingly."[5]

This is the expansive spirit in which Thoreau greets Walden's forest creatures from the axial perspective of his hut, "knowing" each of them in turn as they enter his arc of perception. Though one may remain stationary while experiencing it, familiarization is an act of extending perception—a fact Thoreau acknowledges more fully in "Winter Animals," the chapter that is the counterpart to "Brute Neighbors." In "Winter Animals," the whole environment of the Pond is made proximate: "Walden . . . was my yard" (271). Here we witness the process (now more difficult, but also more transparent, because of the starkness of the winter landscape) through which Thoreau perceives, and thus incorporates, the rabbits, squirrels, jays, chickadees, titmice, and sparrows into the world of his "yard." Even the mysterious hooting owl becomes "quite familiar to me at last" (272), the final phrase confirming that familiarization is an active process.

Similarly, the experience of "floating over [Walden's] surface as the zephyr willed" is hardly unengaged. Thoreau, after all, deliberately "paddled [his] boat to the middle" in order to gain a perspective of centrality and serenity. And the reverie with which he is rewarded is described by the powerful oxymoron, "dreaming *awake*" (191; emphasis added). Such wakeful dreaming is what Bugbee calls a "bathing in fluent reality."[6]

Conversely, the drama of the self's engagement in nature that we witness in the loon passage and in "Spring" involves a form of contemplation—a wonderment before the processes of the world: "And so the seasons went rolling on into summer, as one rambles into higher and higher grass" (319). The loon itself becomes an object of contemplation at the conclusion of "Spring," where it joins the phoebe and other gentler birds in a vision of nature's interrelatedness (319). In the end, the contemplative and creative modes of apprehension reflect one another, are part of the same essential activity, and serve a single purpose: they "enact the 'worlding' of the world."

This phrase comes from an essay by Richard Pevear, who uses it in a discussion of the poetry of George Oppen. Pevear places Oppen's work in contrast to the "solipsism of so much of contemporary writing" and understands it as an antidote to the "worldlessness" of the postwar period.[7] It was, of course, a nineteenth-century version of worldlessness—the condition of "quiet desperation" (8)—that sent Thoreau to the Pond to recover *his* world, and *Walden* may be considered the "poem" he wrote toward his recovery. He was, as many have observed, prescient in understanding how the technology and coercive social structures emerging in his time could alienate people from nature and turn them into machines.[8] One of his reasons for going to

Walden, like many another utopian of his day, was to recover the very ground of being, to "world" the world in this quite literal sense.

Thoreau, of course, had his own "solipsism" to overcome: the alienation that results from philosophical idealism, in its privileging of consciousness and subjectivity. Idealism challenged his vividly experienced sense of a vital, organic earth, and at Walden he put it to the test of his experiment in living. By refusing to be un-worlded, he establishes his relevance for our time, especially in his demonstration that perception can bridge the chasm between spirituality and sensory experience. *Walden* is remarkable in its anticipation of the phenomenological position of twentieth-century philosophers such as Maurice Merleau-Ponty: that "immanence and transcendence [meet] in perception." [9]

But Thoreau's relation to contemporary thought should not be overstated. The worlding enacted by *Walden* does not attempt to redress so profound a condition of "worldlessness" as described by Pevear and other commentators upon postwar alienation. Thoreau did not feel as radically dispossessed of the world as many men and women of the late twentieth century. He did not have to confront the concentration camps, the bomb, and modern totalitarianism—the conditions of "terror" that, according to Isaac Rosenfeld, created "an age of enormity" in which individuals are dwarfed before the massive, often incomprehensible, movements of vast nation-states. And one may add to this list of terrors the ecological destruction of our time, which Thoreau only partially foresaw. These are the conditions in which a writer like Oppen, through a poetry of immanence, strives to bring the very world back into being. We may also think of Charles Olson, who struggles in his *Maximus Poems* to "construct" "an actual earth of value." [10]

For Thoreau, it was not necessary to assert the "actuality" of the world or to "construct" it in quite the sense that Olson intends; his earth of value remained in place, at hand, in the very midst of civilization. That his experiment takes place only "a mile from any neighbor" (3) testifies to his confidence in nature's powers of renewal and its accessibility. The problem was not to bring being out of nothingness, but to demonstrate that all the various "worlds" we might inhabit were supported by one world—nature: "There is a solid bottom every where" (330). *Walden's* morning work is to re-mind Thoreau and his neighbors of nature's proximity and importance: "alert and healthy natures *remember* that the sun rose clear" (8; emphasis added). The "restless, nervous, bustling, trivial Nineteenth Century" (329) had obscured, rather than obliterated, nature's centrality to human life, and what was needed was a reorientation, or repositioning, of the self toward the world.

This repositioning occurs steadily throughout the early chapters of *Walden,* and its realization is confirmed in the chapter "The Village," in which Thoreau's almost anthropological analysis of Concord's human structures (168) shows how psychologically distanced from civilization he has become. At this point, he has achieved for himself the state of being he recommends to "pilgrims" in the earlier chapter "Visitors"—to "really [have] left the village behind" (154). His sentient, "dreaming" (170) return to "my snug harbor in the woods" (169) confirms the full relocation of his perspective and prepares us for the "worlding" that occurs so magnificently in the subsequent chapter "The Ponds." *

The point is that, given the proper perspective, the world would "world" itself. Changeless and perennial, like Walden Pond, the world would appear to grow by assuming its true proportions, if we adopted the right mode of apprehension. At Walden, a world gradually comes into being and enlarges as the doors of perception are cleansed through the discipline of solitude. This is the process that occurs in "The Ponds" and, with the different emphasis I have indicated, in the climactic chapter "Spring." In both cases, the "little world" of Walden becomes big, which is to say, as big as it really is: "The universe is wider than our views of it" (*Wa,* 320).

In stressing Walden's expansiveness, I intend to revise somewhat the traditional notion of the Pond as a microcosm. Certainly its various

---

*That not everyone has the capacity to reposition himself in this way, even given the opportunity, is demonstrated in "Higher Laws" by the case of John Farmer (222).

images as " 'God's Drop' " (194), as "crystal" (199), and as "earth's eye" (186) suggest a concentrated or condensed (symbolic) representation of the cosmos. But if, from one point of view, Walden gathers the cosmos, from another point of view, it opens into it; "earth's eye" looks out, and, to the extent that we can align our own vision with that of Walden (itself a cosmos), we may gain a "broad margin" (111) for our lives.[11]

The worlding of Walden is more than anything else a process of dilation, which culminates in the final chapter's images of exploration (320–22), expansion (323), and *"Extra vagance"* (324). We can track the essential movement of *Walden* by shifting our view from the modest hut whose construction is meticulously described in the first chapter, "Economy," to the "cavernous house" (243) of which Thoreau dreams in "House-Warming." This dream-house is a place for dwelling, in the most profound and satisfying sense of this word, and serves as an analogue for the capacious sense of habitation that the world of Walden, as cosmos, offers to Thoreau.

But it is important to remember that this grand house could not have taken imaginative form in *Walden* without Thoreau's having first rendered the building of his hut. Among the many ways in which "Economy" prepares us for the book's subsequent developments, this is the most important. As Martin Heidegger writes, "We attain to dwelling . . . only by means of building." He reminds us that "[t]he Old English and High German word for building, *buan,* means to dwell," "to stay in a place," and that this experience earns for us a sense of "peace" which, in turn, is freeing. Dwelling, which begins with building and the cultivation of the "near," ultimately leads to dwelling "on the earth" and "under the sky."[12]

Thoreau's description of Walden Pond supports this formulation, for immediately after exclaiming, "How peaceful the phenomena of the lake!" (188), he shows how "[it] is intermediate between land and sky" (188–89)—a link to the heavens. And whether or not you attain *"Extra vagance,"* we should remember, "depends on how you are yarded" (324)—depends, that is, on the fact of your *being* yarded.[13]

The process of familiarization by which Walden becomes "my yard" is the necessary preparation for the expansion of spirit and perception celebrated in the "Conclusion."

This observation suggests the way in which Walden is both a closely circumscribed setting and also one of vast, unlimited extension. On the one hand, the Pond is "stoned . . . and fringed . . . with pine woods" (137), and its "horizon [is] bounded by woods" (130). But such boundaries are not, according to Heidegger, necessarily restrictive: "A boundary is not that at which something stops but, as the Greeks recognized, the boundary is that from which something *begins its presencing.*" [14] And such presencing—what we have called worlding—changes our relation to space. As Thoreau writes in describing the transformation that has occurred for him at Walden, "Both place and time were changed, and I dwelt nearer to those parts of the universe and to those eras in history which had most attracted me. Where I lived was as far off as many a region viewed nightly by astronomers" (87–88).*

At Walden, the "interval" between the near and the far (between, for example, the proximate world of Thoreau's hut and the more distant world inhabited by the loon) disappears: "[S]pace as interval," Heidegger writes, becomes "space as pure extension." [15] And when space becomes extension, everything is proximate; we are at home in the universe: "Why should I feel lonely? is not our planet in the Milky Way?" (*Wa*, 133).

When Thoreau recalls, in "The Bean-Field," the Pond as "that fabulous landscape of my infant dreams" (156), he is calling forth the capacious and primary vision of childhood in which, according to Wordsworth, we saw the world as it really is. But the oneiric terms with which Thoreau evokes his childhood vision of Walden show the

*In this chapter, "Where I Lived, and What I Lived For," Thoreau says that in actuality Walden is "somewhat higher than" the village of Concord, but that in imagination it becomes for him "a tarn high up on the side of a mountain, its bottom far above the surface of other lakes" (86). "Where I Lived"—the space that the location called Walden opens to imagination—is a place *extended.*

difficulty of sustaining this vision in adulthood ("civilization").* For him, art is the vehicle through which it may be preserved and re-experienced.[16] We have seen how *Walden* makes a world, how it enacts that process; now we are in a position to see how it attempts to secure the world thus made. Like the mature Journal, it does so by drawing the boundaries of the perceptual category that its phenomena define and fill; it "pictures" the world, specifically by enlarging it. This is the sense in which Walden is "a world of *full* and fair proportions" (emphasis added), a world filled almost to overflowing but ultimately held steadily in place by "the equilibrium of the whole lake" (*Wa,* 187)—by the totality of Thoreau's aesthetic vision.

Thoreau's confidence in his ability to create such a picture of the world is stated in "Where I Lived, and What I Lived For": "it is . . . glorious to carve and paint the very atmosphere and medium through which we look, which morally we can do" (90). When "carved" and "painted," Thoreau's picture of Walden will, he fervently hopes, over-come the "corrosion of time" (102)—exactly the purpose of books as he states it in "Reading." That is, the book called *Walden* will preserve the world of which Walden is "made." His hope for this book is that, like the Artist of Kouroo's staff, it will be "a perfect work [in which] time does not enter" (326).

But, of course, time does enter *Walden*. In "Sounds," Thoreau is "reminded of the lapse of time" (111) by the railroad, according to whose whistle the farmers "set their clocks" (117). Even the idyll of "The Ponds" is interrupted by the "ear-rending neigh" of the "devilish Iron Horse" (192), with all the implications of destructive temporality that this sound conveys. But the force of the book, its desideratum, is exactly that of the Artist of Kouroo: to reveal that "the former lapse of time had been an illusion" (327). From beginning to end, the illusory nature of time and change is what *Walden* seeks to prove. And the great chapter "Spring," with its affirmation of the smoothly running

---

*There are several examples in *Walden* of Thoreau's own failure to do so. His accidental discovery, in "House-Warming," of the groundnut—the "fabulous fruit" of his youth—prompts this reaction: "I had begun to doubt if I had ever dug and eaten [it] in childhood, as I had told, and had not dreamed it" (239).

axle of the universe, the circle of time in which all change is contained
("[a]nd so the seasons went rolling on" [319]), shows how much
Walden shares the spatial vision of the mature Journal.*

But, in its desire to bring time under control, *Walden* also exhibits
its relation to *A Week.* Its method, however, is different from that of
the earlier work, a difference signaled by the pun, "My days were not
days of the week" (112). As I pointed out in discussing Thoreau's first
book, its voyaging in time is essentially linear—encountering time's
discrete manifestations as the voyagers touch different points along the
shores of the Concord and the Merrimack rivers. The voyaging of
Walden, by contrast, is that of "great-*circle* sailing" (320; emphasis
added), a voyaging circumscribed by the boundaries of a pond but spiraling outward to the Milky Way.

In one of Thoreau's several mythological renderings of Walden's origins, he speculates in this way: "in some other geological period it may
have flowed [in the Concord River], and by a little digging, which God
forbid, it can be made to flow thither again" (194). If, in *A Week,*
Thoreau addressed the problem of time by entering its stream, in
Walden he chooses a body of water cut away, isolated and protected,
from that stream, "without any visible inlet or outlet" (175). This
Pond, as Thoreau puns, is "*Walled-in*" (183).†

It is in the nature of *Walden* as a pastoral that the river of time runs
dangerously near and that the Pond's integrity is vulnerable to the ero-
sion ("digging") of time. Walden, of course, is even more immediately
vulnerable to that aggressive tributary of "progress," the railroad,
which "has infringed on its border" (192). Pastorals are always defined
by what they exclude and by the tensions or "interruptions" they ex-

---

*The Pond, Thoreau writes in "Spring," measures "the *absolute* progress of the
season" (299; emphasis added), replacing the railroad as timekeeper. The image of
the great wheel of the seasons is implicit everywhere in this chapter, as, for example, in the pun I have italicized in the following passage: "As every season seems
best to us *in its turn,* so the coming in of spring is like the creation of Cosmos out
of Chaos, and the realization of the Golden Age" (313).

†An analogue is the Hollowell farm, "half a mile from the nearest neighbor, and
separated from the highway by a broad field[,] . . . protected . . . by its fogs from
frosts" (83).

hibit in the act of excluding. What ultimately preserves pastorals like Walden from their contingent dangers is not only their spatial isolation—the boundaries they maintain—but also the language in which they are rendered.

In "The Pond in Winter," pieces of Walden's ice are "carried off" (296) in the railroad cars, after they have been cut and stacked by a small army of workers. But this apparently destructive activity, accompanied by "a peculiar shriek from the locomotive" (295), leaves the Pond intact. Walden, according to Thoreau, remains uninjured for three reasons: only a small portion of the ten thousand tons of stacked ice is actually removed and "[t]hus the pond recovered the greater part" (296); the cutting itself was brief, lasting only sixteen days, and left Walden the same "pure sea-green" (297) vision of solitude it had always been; and finally, the ice that was removed has "mingled with the sacred water of the Ganges," thus allowing Thoreau symbolically to "meet the servant of the Brahmin," whose bucket "grate[s] together in the same well" (298) with his.

In our own age of vast ecological destruction, the first two reasons are not very compelling. A more efficient ice-cutting industry might well have hauled away a larger portion of the Pond; and the brief harvest of 1846–47 might in another year have greatly extended itself, if the activity had proved profitable. Thoreau, of course, knew this; in other writings, he demonstrates his certain knowledge that the natural world could be permanently damaged by industrial and technological forces. But it is in the nature of *Walden,* as a pastoral, largely to diminish this threat, or, rather, to overcome it through the power of rhetoric.[17] This is why Thoreau's final reason for Walden's preservation, so purely fanciful, is also the most compelling. The water—and world—of Walden is convincingly preserved in this chapter through an act of imagination.

The transference of Walden's water to that of the Ganges is an example of the relational imagination at work, reaching all the way around the earth to connect the diverse things of this world. It is a part of *Walden*'s pervasive verbal extravagance, and the buoyant flight of the imagination that it exhibits should remind us of the loon passage.

In that equally extravagant passage, a man and a loon dance a world into being. Yet, as we saw, their dance is performed against the background of the world of Walden, a world already "made," which is to say, prepared—rounded into a preexisting and enduring category of perception. The loon passage dramatizes, grandly, the way in which *Walden* is an expression of both the relational and the categorical imaginations. In biographical terms, this passage shows us that when Thoreau went to Walden he already knew the "shape" of what he would find there. More important, it shows us what he "made" of that world.

≋

six

CONJURING
THE PAST

I f "Brute Neighbors" dramatizes and celebrates the act of dwelling, then "Former Inhabitants" does the opposite. This section of
Walden (the first half of the two-part chapter "Former Inhabitants; and Winter Visitors") describes failed acts of habitation; its setting is a landscape of ruins. And the description of these ruins and
their former inhabitants is framed in such a way as to trivialize them.
The primary reason for considering them, Thoreau announces near
the beginning of the section, is simply to pass the time during the
winter months: "For human society I was obliged to conjure up the
former inhabitants of these woods" (256).

That Thoreau is "obliged" to bring these figures to mind suggests an
indifference to them. Unlike the animals and birds of "Brute Neighbors," whose presence (and presencing) is constitutive of Walden,
these figures must be forced into being, admitted into a world in which
they do not belong. Quite decidedly, the world of Walden's former inhabitants does not world itself, but must be "conjured." The clear implication of these two chapters, when set side by side, is that "brute"

neighbors belong integrally to the natural world, whereas human neighbors, even those long since departed, do not. Like Whitman in "Song of Myself," Thoreau would "turn and live with animals" (sec. 32).

"Former Inhabitants" is thus consistent with *Walden*'s posture toward the human world, which generally is to exclude that world and, when admitting it, to do so selectively and entirely on Thoreau's own terms. (This posture is an important aspect of Walden as an axial site and as a pastoral environment—it filters and absorbs only what it wants from the world beyond its boundaries.) The best society, the richest discourse with an-other, is found between the solitary self and nature—this is the essential point of *Walden* throughout.

If we consider each chapter title of *Walden* an "opening" through which various activities (reading, hoeing beans, practicing solitude) are included and validated as salutary aspects of moral reform, then very little of the human world is welcome here. Only "Visitors" and "Former Inhabitants; and Winter Visitors" specifically invite human beings into Walden, and in each case the presence of the guests serves as much to provide negative examples of society as to provide companionship. Even Therien, that most natural of men, is found wanting for his lack of reflectiveness. This essentially negative purpose for the inclusion of the human seems to apply to the human past as well, as suggested by the closing paragraphs of the "Former Inhabitants" section:

> Alas! how little does the memory of these human inhabitants enhance the beauty of the landscape! Again, perhaps, Nature will try, with me for a first settler, and my house raised last spring to be the oldest in the hamlet.
>
> I am not aware that any man has ever built on the spot which I occupy. Deliver me from a city built on the site of a more ancient city, whose materials are ruins, whose gardens cemeteries. The soil is blanched and accursed there, and before that becomes necessary the earth itself will be destroyed. With such reminiscences I repeopled the woods and lulled myself asleep. [264]

Thoreau has brought these former inhabitants to mind, and into his book, in order to clear the Walden site of the human past. He acknowledges their earlier presence only, it would seem, to banish that presence, thus preparing the ground for his attempt to make an original (Edenic) relation to the universe. The attitude expressed here toward predecessors is the same as that of "Economy," where "[o]ld people" and [o]ld deeds" (8)—Emerson's hated "tradition"—are rejected so that Thoreau may embark upon his own experiment, free of the predecessors' (useless) advice: "Practically, the old have no very important advice to give the young, their own experience has been so partial, and their lives have been such miserable failures" (9).

We are, apparently, to recognize the failed inhabitants of Walden and their ruined dwellings as an illustrative counterpoint to true, enduring settlement. Like Thoreau, they lack material resources (two, for example, are slaves and one is a squatter), but unlike him, they fail to sustain themselves on their meager holdings. Thoreau's poverty, unlike theirs, is voluntary—an experiment showing how little may be required to meet the true "necessaries of life" (11). These former inhabitants reveal their limited capacity for habitation in order that we might see more clearly the profound capacities of the Walden hero—the Pond's rightful "first settler"—to make a world of Walden.

But the problem with this closing passage, so confidently dismissive, is that the previous nine pages—the entire body of "Former Inhabitants"—has been given to a sustained, deeply engaged (and engaging) "repeopl[ing of] the woods." The trivializing frame in which this material has been set is not convincing. "Former Inhabitants" shows us the ghosts of *Walden,* those failed inhabitants who ought not to be important but somehow are. In a book whose posture does not "admit" failure, they have been admitted.

The structure of "Former Inhabitants" is visual and perspectival, its point of view that of a surveyor. The leading sentence of every paragraph introducing a former inhabitant (except the last of these, a special case) situates the viewer topographically: "East of my bean-field, across the road" (257); "Here, by the very corner of my field, still nearer to town" (257); "Down the road, on the right hand" (257); "Farther down the hill, on the left" (258); "Nearer to the town, you come to . . ." (258); "Once more, on the left" (261); "Farther in the woods than any of these" (261).

The movement described by these phrases is random. There is no clear progression, for example, toward "the town" or away from it, and no other principle for spatial ordering clearly emerges. Instead, the viewer-narrator moves about in the environment of Walden arbitrarily, even waywardly—first here, then there. This is a very different kind of motion from that of the dance of man and loon in "Brute Neighbors," where everything works toward a vision of organic unity.

From one point of view, this kind of movement befits the ruins and remnants that are the viewer's objects of perception. They are not integrated spatially because their status in the life of Walden is itself fragmentary. These former inhabitants were, in every sense, marginal people; they do not make themselves available for visual integration, nor, it would seem, does Thoreau wish to integrate them, which is to say, embrace them within his developing pastoral vision of the Pond. Like the frame in which the former inhabitants' stories are set, the overt structure of their narration suggests the author's obligatory, even perfunctory, relation to them.

But if the surveying perspective further diminishes the significance of the former inhabitants, it gives the surveyor authority, makes him a "guide"; his demonstrated visual command of the landscape ("my bean-field") confirms his appropriation of Walden as his "yard." By implication, this perspective also supports the narrator's authority as a guide through Walden's past; it warrants his role as historian (and storyteller) of the former inhabitants' impoverished lives and of their sometimes tragic ends.

The first former inhabitant to be described, Cato Ingraham, was a slave whose dwelling was built for him by his master (unlike the hut that Thoreau "had built [him]self" [4]), and all that remains of it is a "half-obliterated cellar hole" (257), concealed by a "fringe of pines" and known only to a few. The site is but dimly recalled by the community: "There are a few who remember his little patch among the walnuts, which he let grow up till he should be old and need them; but a younger and whiter speculator got them at last" (257). Servitude and victimage are the reasons for the disappearance of Cato's dwelling, but this disappearance apparently is not lamented by Thoreau: "[The cellar hole] is *now* [emphasis added] filled with the smooth sumach, (*Rhus galbra,*) and one of the earliest species of golden-rod (*Solidago stricta*) grows there luxuriantly" (257).

Unlike *A Week,* where the narrative structure "then and now" serves often to memorialize a valued human past, *Walden* more often uses this structure to show nature's vigorous capacity to overtake and replace the human world—a theme inherited by Thoreau from earlier American writers and artists such as Bryant and Cole. "Then" is the failed human past; "now" is the moment of nature's resurgence, a moment of present-ness ("the nick of time") offering the possibility of a new beginning. The dominance of this theme in *Walden* is one of the things that distinguishes it from *A Week,* whose vision of experience is more deeply retrospective. In *Walden,* the human past is generally set aside to open the possibility of a purely prospective stance toward experience.

The second former inhabitant to be described, "Zilpha, a colored woman," is not a slave, and her dwelling—a "little house"—was more substantial and better grounded than that of Cato Ingraham. But it has nevertheless suffered destruction: "[I]n the war of 1812, her dwelling was set on fire by English soldiers, . . . and her cat and dog and hens were all burned up together." The image of conflagration rendered here ("all burned up") is one of utter devastation, and all that remains of Zilpha's presence in these woods is a few "bricks amid the oak copse" and the sound of her singing as it is remembered by "[o]ne old frequenter of these woods" (257).

Here too we may, if we wish, see nature (its sturdy oaks) overtaking a merely human dwelling. But in this case Thoreau does not emphasize the point. Instead, the focus is on Zilpha herself—her victimage before the unpredictable and unavoidable destruction of war, as well as her "hard" and "inhumane" life—and on the act of remembering her: "One old frequenter of these woods *remembers*" (257; emphasis added). Though "loud" and "shrill," her lingering song is "notable." Music almost always figures for Thoreau as a vehicle of transcendence and continuity (the telegraph harp, so often celebrated in the Journal, for example), and Zilpha's voice sings to us from the vanished past. At this point in Thoreau's account of Walden's former inhabitants, we seem to have entered a more fully human world, more sentiently experienced.

Like Cato Ingraham, the former inhabitant described next by Thoreau is a black slave, Brister Freeman, and he is remembered principally through the grove of apple trees he planted. If the sumac and goldenrod that overtook Cato's dwelling and the oaks that replaced Zilpha's house demonstrate nature's endurance beyond merely human structures, these apple trees have a very different purpose in the narrative. A domesticated species, the apple tree does not supplant the human world, it furthers it. "Brister planted and tended" these trees, and because of him they "grow still" (257)—"large old trees now, but their fruit still wild and ciderish to my taste" (257–58).[1] Like Zilpha's song, and like the apple tree at Tyngsborough described in *A Week,* Brister's grove represents continuity from the past into the present and also a union of the natural and the human worlds.

Unlike the stories of Cato and Zilpha, that of Brister involves no mediating "rememberers." Thoreau's knowledge of him may derive from others, but he does not mention them, thus giving himself the role of principal "witness" in this case. It is he, the first-person narrator, who observes ("tastes") Brister's legacy to Walden, and because of this we feel closer to Brister and to his lost world than we did to Cato and Zilpha.

This sense of proximity is intensified and ritualized by Thoreau's visit to "the old Lincoln burying-ground," where he reads the inscription on Brister's gravestone (258). The "unmarked graves" of British soldiers beside Brister's leave their identity unknown, but his grave marks his name distinctly, if disparagingly: "his epitaph . . . styled [him] 'Sippio Brister,'—Scipio Africanus he had some title to be called,—'a man of color,' as if he were discolored. It also told me, with staring emphasis, when he died; which was but an indirect way of informing me that he ever lived" (258).

Even as it marks his identity, Brister's gravestone in an obscure corner of the Lincoln burying-ground leaves his claim on human memory tenuous, drawing into question the significance of his presence at Walden and on the earth. Thoreau's ritual remembrance of him thus becomes all the more important and suggests the deeper redemptive level of psychic activity present in "Former Inhabitants."

The story of Brister Freeman concludes with an apparently gratuitous detail: "With him dwelt Fenda, his hospitable wife, who told fortunes, yet pleasantly" (258). That Brister had a wife—a family—distinguishes him from the solitary figures of Cato and Zilpha (and from Thoreau himself). The portrait of a family living at Walden is developed further in the next site to be described, where Thoreau finds "marks of some homestead of the Stratton family" (258). The image of a "homestead," farmed by a family, alters Walden's past, adds to it the dimension of community.

But the Strattons, like all the other former inhabitants, are doomed. Their "orchard once covered all the slope of Brister's hill, but was long since killed out by pitch-pines, excepting a few stumps" (258). Here the phrasing ("killed out") suggests a different and darker perspective on nature's displacement of the human world than we saw in the description of the luxuriant goldenrod that grows on the site of Cato Ingraham's dwelling. And the stumps scattered on this hillside demonstrate that not every orchard has the enduring power of Brister Freeman's.

The death of the Strattons' orchard figures their own death—the failure of their experiment to endure—and in the following paragraph (which introduces a new site, "Breed's location") we find the description of a "mythological character . . . who first comes in the guise of a friend or hired man, and then robs and murders the whole family" (258). As in the stories of illness and death that emerge in Huckleberry Finn's artful lies, we may wish to see in this fanciful rendering of Walden's history a deep-seated fear of the death of families, which is to say, of human generativity. And we begin to sense that Thoreau may be as concerned, at some level, with this form of generativity as he is with nature's.

To see "Former Inhabitants" in this light is to give as much emphasis to the second word of the title as to the first. These accounts describe not only the failure but the possibility of inhabiting; behind all of them lies the fear that Thoreau's own act of habitation may fail.[2] Necessarily, this fear involves his understanding that—for all that he invests in solitude and self-reliance—his own attempt to inhabit Walden cannot finally be detached from the larger human enterprise of "settlement."

The other legend associated with Breed's location is that of a tavern: "Here once a tavern stood; the well the same, which tempered the traveller's beverage and refreshed his steed. Here then men saluted one another, and heard and told the news, and went their ways again" (258). Though the legend has but "dubious" (258) foundation, Thoreau's inclusion of it—with its images of warm conviviality—at this point in the narrative supports the theme of human community that has been developing in the interstices of his narration.[3]

The legends with which Breed's location is associated mark a shift in the narration of "Former Inhabitants"; we are moving from what is known more or less "historically" about Walden to the realm of "old mythology" (258). The legendary murderer in disguise and the ghostly tavern are elements that Washington Irving might have included in his "repeopling" of the Hudson River valley. But the account of Breed's location pauses only briefly on these Irvingesque materials, moving quickly to a still deeper level of storytelling—from legend to personal mythology.

The phrase "Breed's location" is an empty signifier that not only implies the transience of Breed's presence but also opens the site to whatever values and "myths" the imagination may attach to it. Breed's "hut" is an architectural structure of similarly open, undesignated value. Though it "was standing only a dozen years ago, . . . it had [even then] long been unoccupied" (259). That Thoreau says of this empty hut, "[i]t was about the size of mine," implies an invidious distinction between this structure and his own hut, so richly filled with fruitful acts of habitation. But at a deeper level, Breed's hut *is* Thoreau's; its emptiness awaits his filling it. This neutral "location" and this "un-occupied" hut open themselves for the telling of Thoreau's own story.

The narrative that follows—the longest and most sustained of any of the inhabitants' stories—takes us back a dozen years to a winter night when Thoreau, having "just lost [him]self over Davenant's Gondibert" and beset by "a lethargy," is suddenly roused to action:

> I had just sunk my head on this when the bells rung fire, and in hot haste the engines rolled that way, led by a straggling troop of men and boys, and I among the foremost, for I had leaped the brook. We thought it was far south over the woods,—we who had run to fires before,—barn, shop, or dwelling house, or all together. "It's Baker's barn," cried one. "It is the Codman Place," affirmed another. And then fresh sparks went up above the wood, as if the roof fell in, and we all shouted "Concord to the rescue!" [259]

Thoreau has been awakened from his passivity into alertness, but for the reader the movement dramatized in this passage is from one form of dream ("lethargy") to another—a dream-remembrance of youthful adventure characterized by "leaping," camaraderie, and ex-citement.* (The episode reminds us of the adventuring in *A Week,* and John Thoreau's presence can be felt in the deep background of the story.) The spirit of adventure continues in the aftermath of the fire, which, for all of Thoreau's and his companions' plans to "throw a frog-pond" on it, destroys Breed's hut: "So we stood round our engine, jostled one another, expressed our sentiments through speaking trum-pets, or in lower tone referred to the great conflagrations which the

---

*Thoreau read Davenant's "Gondibert" in the early 1840s, when he was a young adult (see Sattelmeyer, *Thoreau's Reading,* 32–33). But, as incorporated in this pas-sage, the episode (both the reading, which has about it the sense of "homework," and the adventure that frees Thoreau from his mental labors) calls up the spirit of adolescence.

world has witnessed. . . . We finally retreated without doing any mischief" (260). But the mischief has been done. At the very beginning of this story, we learned that Breed's hut "was set on fire by mischievous boys." Indeed, it is later rumored that "they who set the fire . . . gave the alarm" (259). Surely, this double role characterizes Thoreau as well; he would both destroy this "worthless" (260) dwelling and save it.

These are the polar impulses at work in "Former Inhabitants," and in *Walden* as a whole. The fiery destruction of Breed's hut echoes the destruction of Zilpha's house and figures symbolically in the same way, clearing the Walden site for Thoreau's own experiment at the Pond but also reflecting his fears for the destruction of his own hut, which is to say, his being. (Fire, in its capacity to destroy utterly, belongs in his imagination to the "Rough.") Thoreau, however, plays the parts here not only of arsonist and fireman, but also of "survivor." The night following the conflagration, he returns (alone now) to the site of the smoldering ruin. Despite the following passage's opening phrase, there is nothing fortuitous about his return; in the deepest sense, it is purposeful:

> It chanced that I walked that way across the fields the following night about the same hour, and hearing a low moaning at this spot, I drew near in the dark, and discovered the only survivor of the family that I know, the heir of both its virtues and its vices, who alone was interested in this burning, lying on his stomach and looking over the cellar wall at the still smouldering cinders beneath, muttering to himself, as is his wont. He had been working far off in the river meadows all day, and had improved the first moments that he could call his own to visit the home of his fathers and his youth. [260]

In this figure of the "heir" who returns to "the home of his fathers and his youth" only to find it destroyed, we surely have the doppelgänger. Here the self gazes at the self in the act of gazing:

> He gazed into the cellar from all sides and points of view by turns, always lying down to it, as if there was some treasure,

which he remembered, concealed between the stones, where
there was absolutely nothing but a heap of bricks and ashes. The
house being gone, he looked at what there was left. [260]

This passage records a response to devastation, to profound loss.
The scene dramatizes the loss of history and family ("the home of his
fathers") and of one's own past within the family ("his youth"), and
it shows the risks of destroying, or severing, such relations. They are
the "treasure" that cannot be found, and the perspectival method
("gaz[ing] . . . from all sides and points of view by turns"), which so
efficaciously "worlded" the world in "Brute Neighbors," is here un-
availing. As a parable, the destruction of Breed's hut and the witnessing
of its ruin show the costs of going it alone, of detaching oneself from the
human community and withdrawing from human history—from those
predecessors so firmly rejected on the early pages of "Economy." [4]

Breed's hut is, on one level, Thoreau's own hut, a symbol of his brave
experiment in self-reliance. But it is also the hut of the breed, the species, the tribe, the race, the human family. Similarly, the story of Breed's
location is Thoreau's story set among the stories of others who were
there before him. He has displaced them, but he is of them, their
"heir"—part of the same "family." The narrative structure of "Former
Inhabitants," with Thoreau's own story deep in its center, unmistakably carries this implication. And, as the closing line in the following
passage makes clear, it is precisely "the history of a family" (261) that is
at stake in "Former Inhabitants":

> He was soothed by the sympathy which my mere presence im-
> plied, and showed me, as well as the darkness permitted, where
> the well was covered up; which, thank Heaven, could never be
> burned; and he groped long about the wall to find the well-
> sweep which his father had cut and mounted, feeling for the iron
> hook or staple by which a burden had been fastened to the heavy
> end,—all that he could now cling to,—to convince me that it
> was no common "rider." I felt it, and still remark it almost daily
> in my walks, for by it hangs the history of a family. [260–61]

This iron hook is exactly analogous to the nail in the apple tree at Tyngsborough described in *A Week*. It is a remnant of the human past, a symbol of continuity between "then" and "now," a way of remembering what would otherwise be forgotten. The heir's "groping" for the hook symbolizes the difficulty of this process, and the "sympathy" that Thoreau extends to him is a gesture toward remaking the human connections that have been broken. Insofar as the well is cognate with Walden Pond (like Walden, it is indestructible), the Pond shifts its meanings from those emphasized in "Brute Neighbors" and "The Ponds." If, from one point of view, Walden opens outward to the cosmos, worlding the world in this sense, it also provides the setting around which human community may form—showing its potential relation to the river valleys of *A Week*. Thoreau's imagined role as "first settler" implies further settlement.[5]

Like a well, Walden is a deep repository of human value—"the work of a brave man . . . [who] rounded this water with his hand, deepened and clarified it in his thought, and in his will bequeathed it to Concord" (193). But unlike the well at Breed's location, it cannot be "covered up" (except by its own "skin"); and unlike the lifeless ruins depicted in this chapter, its story cannot be silenced. Thoreau's implicit work in "Former Inhabitants" is the uncovering of wells, which means, in part, discovering the underground connection between them and the Pond—the connection between society and nature. To make this connection would restore to these ruins their former vitality; it would be the first step in their reconstruction.

Reconstruction is indeed the work of "Former Inhabitants." Or perhaps it would be more accurate to say that its various stories are gestures toward the reconstruction of prior worlds. By telling the stories of the former inhabitants, Thoreau reimagines (re-images) them for the reader, thereby witnessing for their existence. He would have us know that Cato's and Zilpha's vanished dwellings once stood here and, if possible, would have us see them as well. He would have us know that on this hillside scattered with stumps once existed the Strattons' orchard, and he envisions it through remembrance.

The imaginative reconstruction of ruins is a central activity of the mature Journal. Throughout the decade of the 1850s, we find Thoreau searching the landscape of Concord and of other parts of New England for its buried origins. In March 1859, for example, he discovered within the wreckage of Concord's recently destroyed Hunt House evidence of another, older house—the Winthrop house—which "go[es] back to near the settlement of the town" (*J*, 12:37). The inscription of a date on the now-exposed chimney, an English coin, chalk-writing on the timbers—these provide the basis for Thoreau's reconstruction. Through his powers of deduction, in which he expresses much pride ("Consider how I discovered . . ."), he learns even "where the Winthrop family . . . placed their front door two hundred years ago" (*J*, 12:59).

More important than Thoreau's powers of deduction, however, is the fact that the old Winthrop house (even its delicate chalk marks, which were almost immediately washed away by the rain when exposed [*J*, 12:47]) was protected for many decades by its encasement within another house. Like the inhabitants of the decayed village of Billerica, whose ruins are visited in *A Week,* the Winthrops left behind a record of their life—a record preserved amazingly intact. And the New Englanders who followed them have, in effect, preserved their relation to the Winthrops—and to the past they represent—by building their own house around the ancient house. This image, a home within a home, a past within the present, is one of profound continuity.

None of this is true of the ruins in "Former Inhabitants," which have long been exposed to the elements and whose inscriptions have washed away. In this sense, they are akin to the Indians' lost culture, the "ashes of [whose] unchronicled nations" (158) Thoreau disturbs while hoeing in "The Bean-Field." Like those of the Indians, the ruins of "Former Inhabitants" are so fragmentary, so far "gone," that there is almost nothing for the reconstructive imagination to work with—a stray brick, a stump, sometimes nothing at all. As Thoreau writes in his overview of Walden's ruins:

> These cellar dents, like deserted fox burrows, old holes, are all that is left where once were the stir and bustle of human life, and

"fate, free-will, foreknowledge absolute," in some form and dialect or other were by turns discussed. But *all I can learn* of their conclusions amounts to just this, that "Cato and Brister pulled wool;" which is about as edifying as the history of more famous schools of philosophy. [263; emphasis added]

How different is the defeated tone of this passage from the confident claims Thoreau makes in summarizing his reconstruction of the Winthrop house. Our view of the past, as rendered in "Former Inhabitants," is fragmentary because the objects of perception are themselves fragments. The halting movement of the narrator, stepping first here and then there, is the movement of an archaeologist. Its apparent randomness suggests a strenuous, faltering attempt to find one's way among the ruins, to "grope" toward some viable perspective on the past, to make something of these remnants.

This is a different kind of "making" from that of "Brute Neighbors," where a world is made through a process of spatial dilation. Here, the Walden hero attempts to make a world through the difficult process of synthesis and reconstruction—a temporal process much more akin to that of *A Week* than to that of *Walden*. In "Brute Neighbors," and in *Walden* as a whole, visual observation is an expansive process; in "Former Inhabitants," on the other hand, visual observation is focused, particularized. Rather than dilation, we have what might be called refraction—a process by which the past is "seen" prismatically, inferentially. Analogously, the narrator's dependence on the stories of witnesses, through whom he learns the design of some of the vanished structures, suggests a secondary, filtered appropriation of the world rather than the dramatic, unmediated vision of the world in "Brute Neighbors."

Because the world of "Former Inhabitants" will not world itself, it must be "conjured," in a much more important sense than Thoreau's trivializing context for this word suggests. That is, the lost human world of Walden must be reconstructed, synthesized, from its meager, scattered remnants. And the elements of this synthesis are not only bricks and cellar holes. They include the myths that belong to these sites, such as the "mythological character" and the "tavern" associated with Breed's location. Myth must substitute for fact in the making of this composite vision, since there is so little to work with. Like the shaman, Thoreau must bring this world back into being through dream and incantation.

Yet, in a larger sense, the process of rebuilding the lost world of Walden's former inhabitants is inherently mythic. Myth—and this includes Thoreau's personal myth as it weaves through the narrative—is the binding force of reconstruction holding his reimagined world in place. It is also his means of establishing a humanly felt connection to that world. Speaking of the sad history of Breed's location, Thoreau writes: "[H]istory must not yet tell the tragedies enacted here; let time intervene in some measure to assuage and lend an azure tint to them" (258). Myth, as an "assuaging" force, is analogous to the "sympathy" Thoreau extends to the heir of Breed's hut. From one point of view, this sympathy softens the harshness of history—the glare of the "real"—but from another, it is sympathy that makes contact possible. Myth not only provides an "assuaging" distance; it also provides a way in, and back.

The work of synthesizing fragments, stories, and myths toward the formation of a composite vision, as we saw in *A Week,* belongs to art—the art of memory, in a sense different from that of the Journal. And as Thoreau moves on from Breed's location to a new site, he offers a parable illustrating the point. This site, "[f]arther in the woods than any of [the others]" (261), belonged to Wyman the potter, who "furnished his townsmen with earthen ware, and left descendants to succeed him" (261). Wyman is the only former inhabitant whose descendants are mentioned and about whom one senses some kind of continuing presence in the Walden environment. He owes that presence to his role as artisan:

> I had read of the potter's clay and wheel in Scripture, but it had never occurred to me that the pots we use were not such as had come down *unbroken* from those days . . . , and I was pleased to hear that so *fictile* an art was ever practised in my neighborhood. [261; emphases added]

The most important "fictile" art practiced in Thoreau's neighborhood is, of course, his own. It takes the "broken" images of the past and molds them in a new configuration—"revising mythology" (269). And this "fictile" art, as it is specifically practiced in "Former Inhabitants," is also "fictive"; it is the art of storytelling. Narrative, as embodied in story and myth, is the force that holds together the fragments of "Former Inhabitants." This is a different kind of art from that which, in "The Ponds" or "Brute Neighbors," fixes Walden for us as an indelible, pictorial image transcending time. Earthenware is of the earth and is to be distinguished from the immutable landscape painting that *Walden* presents to the mind's eye. Wyman's pots are different from the Artist of Kouroo's staff; they can be broken. As artifacts, they belong to daily life, which finally wears them out.

That is to say, the art of narrative is a temporal art; all stories are stories of lives, and lives exist in time. This is another way in which the "Former Inhabitants" section of *Walden* shows its relation to *A Week,* where the journey structure involves its voyagers and its readers in the flow of time and the wreckage of history. *Walden,* on the whole, does not involve us in this way. Its temporal location is the nick of time (the instant of promise, possibility, and renewal) or, from another perspective, the eternal present. Its events are not measurable along a continuum, but are archetypal and symbolic. As we have seen, *Walden*'s chapter organization is essentially topical ("Reading," "Solitude") and spatial ("The Bean-Field," "The Ponds"), and its larger seasonal structure is based upon an immutable spatial image—the circle of time. This structure determines the book's development and prevents it from ever settling into a temporal, narrative mode for very long.

Though "stories" have an important place in the more open, occasional form of the Journal (it is here that Thoreau the local colorist emerges most clearly)[6] and in the digressive, discursive structure of *A Week, Walden* does not make much room for them. Its tight synthesis of elements and its forceful thematic emphases tend to interrupt narrative developments before they gain momentum. When stories do appear, they are usually brief and enigmatic "parables," like the story of the bug in the table's dry leaf, that serve primarily to illustrate the book's themes. Stories generally require greater amplitude of context than *Walden* provides and a larger platform for action. The stationary, solitary hero of Walden Pond has few of the possibilities for adventure and social encounter that we find, for example, in *A Week*—a story that carries us upon two rivers into regions far beyond Walden.

By sustaining the narrative mode longer than any other chapter in *Walden,* "Former Inhabitants" provides the largest "opening" through which the human past (history) may enter the timeless world of the Pond. And even though this opening is framed by a trivializing context and the narration itself is heavily mediated by authorial commentary, the cumulative effect of these stories told one after another, over the span of nine pages, is to stress the force of temporality. The differing contents and emphases of the individual stories are less important, from this perspective, than their verbal action. Taken together, they enact the force and flow of time, acknowledging its inevitable presence even in the Edenic world of Walden.

Their work, in other words, is to introduce the theme of *Et in Arcadia ego.* The fictile-fictive art of "Former Inhabitants" leads us into time and toward time's ultimate manifestation, death. Death is where the story of a life must lead and where "Former Inhabitants" takes us. All the former inhabitants, of course, are dead; they belong to a dead, and deadened, world. But with the next inhabitant, Hugh Quoil, comes an enactment of death ("He died in the road" [262]) and a most particular sense of terminus. The passage introducing him begins, "The last inhabitant of these woods before me was an Irishman, Hugh Quoil" (261). Quoil is the only one of the former inhabitants initially identified through his temporal rather than spatial location in the world of Walden. We learn soon enough where he lived—he "occupied Wyman's tenement" (261–62)—but the most important thing about him is that he is the last.

The positioning of Quoil's story in "Former Inhabitants" confirms what we have been only vaguely sensing up to this point in the narrative: that while the stories do not follow in a strict chronological order (their disorder is an aspect of fragmentation), the force of history does indeed push them along. Just beneath the overt spatial organization of the chapter—the narrator moving here and there through the Walden landscape—lies a deeper principle of organization: from Walden's past to its present—to Thoreau's own "time." The stories are taking us toward the pivotal moment when the end and the beginning meet, when the old world of Walden's former inhabitants disappears completely and the new world of Thoreau's fresh experiment takes life.

The death of Quoil gathers and represents the deaths of all the former inhabitants and brings their influence upon the Walden landscape to a close. That his house was "pulled down" reminds us of the destruction of Zilpha's house; his "broken" pipe and other effects, "scattered over the floor" (262), have their counterparts in the remnants of Breed's hut; and the "dim outline of [his] garden" belongs with the Strattons' failed orchard. Finally, "the trembling delirium" that killed him represents the debilitating anxiety, the dis-ease, that plagues human beings in society. The sense of ruin at this site, its garden "overrun with Roman wormwood and beggar-ticks" (262), attaches to the whole world of Walden's former inhabitants and, at a farther remove, to the larger world of human society from which Thoreau has withdrawn. As he writes in "The Bean-Field," "[t]he true husbandman [which he hopes to become at Walden] will cease from anxiety" (166).

Yet Quoil, as Thoreau represents him, is a "tragic" figure—"a man of manners, . . . capable of more civil speech than you could well attend to" (262)—and if we find him representative of the other former inhabitants, then his tragedy is theirs and, potentially, Thoreau's own. For the story of Quoil not only recapitulates the failures of the past; it also anticipates the possible failures of the future. This is the other, and more important, sense in which the story of Hugh Quoil is pivotal.

Thoreau's "visit" to Quoil's destroyed house takes the form of an accounting; he and the "administrator" who surveys the scene are one. His viewing of the "old clothes curled up by use," the broken pipe, and the "soiled [playing] cards" is an attempt to tally all the elements of this ruin, as if—taking a lesson from them—they could prevent his own future ruin. Yet there is one object of his vision that cannot be "accounted" for: "One black chicken . . . the administrator could not catch, black as night and as silent, not even croaking" (262).

As "administrator" of Walden's past—its historian and storyteller—Thoreau stands above the ruins, distancing himself from them as he attempts to learn from them. ("[W]hy," he asks later, "did ["this small village"] fail while Concord keeps its ground?" [264].) Yet this black, silent chicken will not be caught. In the end, death cannot be "tallied" and even the most "fictile" of arts cannot contain it. It is the common destiny of all of Walden's inhabitants, former and future, and the common end of all their stories. Mortality is the unavoidable failure of us all; it implies the possibility of failure in all human affairs—even the most "deliberate."

At various moments throughout *Walden,* Thoreau hints at the possible failure of his own experiment. Though it cannot be said that his garden, like Hugh Quoil's, "never received its first hoeing" (262), his most important crop did fail. In "The Bean-Field" he confesses, "I am obliged to say to you, Reader, that the seeds which I planted, if indeed they *were* the seeds of those virtues [sincerity, truth, simplicity, faith, and innocence], were wormeaten or had lost their vitality, and so did not come up" (164). The determined optimism of *Walden* ordains that this admission should be quickly discounted, and only a page later it is replaced by the serene confidence expressed in the following rhetorical question: "How, then, can our harvest fail?" (166).

But *Walden* does "admit" failure, in the margins and the interstices, and most openly in "Former Inhabitants." Implicitly, through parable, this chapter asks: Will my orchard, like the Strattons', be cut down? Will my garden, like Quoil's, be overrun and infested? Will my hut, like the dwellings of Cato, Zilpha, and Breed, be destroyed? Will my experiment, like the settlements of those who went before me, fail to endure? Will it go unmarked and unremembered?

Even the celebratory chapter, "The Ponds," expresses Thoreau's doubts concerning his ability to fully exploit Walden's spiritual advantages: "—Why, here is Walden, the same woodland lake that I discovered so many years ago; . . . it is the same liquid joy and happiness to itself and its Maker, ay, and it *may* be to me" (193).

The emphatic conditional of the above phrase suggests Thoreau's complex sense of the meaning of change. Change meant possibility—

the opportunity for self-renewal such as he tried to give himself at Walden in 1845. But, as his brother's death had taught him only three and a half years earlier, change was a dimension of time, and time could bring loss—profound loss. Because the Pond was "itself unchanged, the same water which my youthful eyes fell on," it was not implicated in time and therefore not subject to loss. It was the measure by which the meaning of change in human affairs could be gauged. And when Thoreau reflects, "all the change is in me" (193), he is contrasting nature's perennial youthfulness and "life" with the attrition and death that inevitably defeat human purposes. Given its context, the phrase can only mean: "All the loss is in me."

The rhetoric of *Walden* works to limit the possibility of loss. By its rhetoric I mean those things that belong generically to the book's pastoral and utopian purposes—its stated program for moral reform, its determined buoyancy, its commitment to the future, its desire to sing like chanticleer and wake Thoreau's neighbors up. These purposes cannot be dismissed as belonging merely to a surface structure; they are an essential, authentic part of Thoreau's morning work and confirm his promise that *Walden* will not be "an ode to dejection" (84).

But, in *Walden,* Thoreau had another kind of morning work to do as well—the work that, in our time, Charles Olson called the archaeology of morning.[7] This is the work of reaching toward origins, toward recovering the "prior." In part, this involves imagining Walden's natural origins, for which Thoreau offers a number of theories both geological and mythic. Clearly, it was as important to him that Walden have a beginning—and therefore an issuance out of a natural past—as that it have a bottom. His desire for continuity, for evolutionary process, demanded this. But the human past was important to him as well, and, unlike the natural past, it often showed not continuity but discontinuity—the breakage and wreckage of history. Once involved in the remembrance of history, he found himself, even in *Walden,* implicated in tragedy and failure.

The whole weight of this implication can be felt in the passage that follows the story of the tragic Hugh Quoil. Lifting the reader out of the past into the present moment of his own experiment ("Now"),

Thoreau gives an overview of Walden's ruins—a vision of "what there was left." In doing this, he acts less the claimant than the mourner:

> Now only a dent in the earth marks the site of these dwellings, with buried cellar stones, and strawberries, raspberries, thimble-berries, hazel-bushes, and sumachs growing in the sunny sward there; some pitch-pine or gnarled oak occupies what was the chimney nook, and a sweet-scented black-birch, perhaps, waves where the door-stone was. Sometimes the well dent is visible, where once a spring oozed; now dry and tearless grass; or it was covered deep,—not to be discovered till some late day,—with a flat stone under the sod, when the last of the race departed. What a sorrowful act that must be,—the covering up of wells! coincident with the opening of wells of tears. [263]

The vision of "Former Inhabitants" is, finally, one of sorrow and sympathy. At its deepest level, it affirms rather than rejects the relation between the past and the present, between predecessors and heirs. Thoreau's deepest wish is to re-member these former inhabitants, and he does so through the same symbol that Whitman would later employ in his remembrance of Lincoln: "Still grows the vivacious lilac, a generation after the door and lintel and the sill are gone, unfolding its sweet-scented flowers each spring . . . ; planted and tended once by children's hands, in front-yard plots,—now standing by wall-sides in retired pastures, and giving place to new-rising forests;—the last of that stirp, sole survivor of that family" (263).

How different is the lilac from the sumac and goldenrod that overtook Cato Ingraham's house. No less "luxuriant" than these wild plants, it reminds us in its continued flowering of those who planted it and is the "sole survivor of that family." Standing halfway between civilization ("front-yard plots") and nature ("new-rising forests"), it links these worlds without losing any of its integrity—"blossoming as fair, and smelling as sweet, as in that first spring." A "half century after [the children who planted it] had grown up and died," the lilac "tell[s] their story faintly to the lone wanderer," giving voice to a human presence otherwise forgotten. In "mark[ing] its still tender, civil, cheerful, lilac colors," Thoreau acknowledges the importance of his own story-telling and of the former inhabitants whose stories he tells (263–64).

~~~~~~~~~

Thoreau first drafted some parts of "Former Inhabitants," in his Journal, during the fall of 1845 and the winter of 1845–46, and, as Robert Sattelmeyer points out, these passages (including those on Hugh Quoil's death) "already have in this earliest version that chapter's elegiac tone" (*PJ,* 2:455). That is, "Former Inhabitants" shares the elegiac spirit in which *A Week* was written during the 1840s. But other portions of "Former Inhabitants," including the stories of Cato, Zilpha, Brister, the Strattons, and, most significantly, that of Breed's hut, were added very late—as late, perhaps, as 1853.[8] From this late perspective, Thoreau had become the "survivor" of his own years at the pond, "gazing" into the ruins of his experience "from all sides and points of view by turns," attempting to see "what there was left." By this time, his own hut was in ruin and had joined the succession of Walden's other ruins. Though his experiment had concluded more de-liberately ("I had several more lives to live") than did those of the others, his "settlement" at the Pond was no more enduring than theirs had been. Thoreau himself had become a former inhabitant, and it is his own past at the Pond with which this chapter is most centrally concerned.

Understood in this way, all of Walden's former inhabitants are ver-sions of the Thoreauvian self: the enslaved self, the besieged and dis-possessed self, the generative self who plants and nurtures (whether it be apple trees or beans), the solitary self, the self who destroys (Thoreau did, after all, set the woods on fire), the self who rescues, the self who has suffered losses and who mourns, the self who remembers and reconstructs, the self who creates, the self who must die. Though part of him would disenfranchise those who preceded him, another part contains, and speaks for, the whole history of Walden; its history is his story. And that story, in turn, is the book called *Walden*—the one enduring "structure" of Thoreau's years at the Pond.

Sherman Paul has written that *Walden,* as a whole, is a fable of renewal.[9] "Former Inhabitants" is, we may say, a counter-fable dramatizing the possibility of failure and the inevitability of loss. It is the place where a powerful but largely submerged crosscurrent of *Walden* surfaces most prominently into view. This crosscurrent, we should remember, was the *main* current of *A Week,* a book whose treatment of loss—both personal and historical—is built into its very structure. But the reverse, of course, is equally true: *A Week* has woven within it several important themes that would surface more prominently in *Walden.* For all its journeying into the wreckage of history, and for all its implicit mourning of John Thoreau's tragic death, *A Week* expresses much joy and high-spiritedness. Though it concludes with autumn, rather than spring, this conclusion—like that of *Walden*—offers hope and the possibility of renewal. The key is lower, the joy more muted, but the similarities are unmistakable.

Further, the differences between the restrospective vision of *A Week* and the prospective vision of *Walden* can be overemphasized. For *Walden,* too, is a book about the past. Its first word is "When," and its first paragraph establishes a temporal frame around the whole of the narration: "When I wrote the following pages, or rather the bulk of them, I lived alone, in the woods. . . . I lived there two years and two months. At present I am a sojourner in civilized life again" (3). All of *Walden* is a memory, an extended remembrance of an experience long since concluded—recreated for the reader by Thoreau's "fictile" art. Though its form discourages extended storytelling, *Walden* is itself a story, commemorating an experience that, like the treasure of Breed's hut, is "gone." *

When viewed in this context, *Walden* appears not as the culmination of Thoreau's career but as a pivotal book—establishing a balance between the mourning work of the 1840s and the pure spatial vision

---

*This does not mean that Thoreau's life in the period following his years at the Pond was unrewarding. To be sure, those years offered him many satisfactions—not the least of which was the pleasure he took in his developing Journal. The point is that, throughout his life, Thoreau's memory of the Walden years remained a vital imaginative resource.

toward which the mature Journal of the 1850s points. It looks backward even as it looks forward.* And how could this not be so? How could *Walden,* begun at the Pond only a few years after the death of John Thoreau, during the period of *A Week*'s major development,[10] not trail loss behind it? And, more broadly, how could a writer with a vision of life so deeply retrospective have excluded the human past and its tragedies from any book he might have written? The question is not whether, but how, loss is treated in *Walden,* and "Former Inhabitants" gives us the answer.

For while this chapter is exceptional in the various ways I have indicated, in this respect it is absolutely characteristic: wherever loss figures in *Walden,* it appears in the interstices and in the form of parable. We need only think of the mysterious story of the lost hound, bay horse, and turtledove to remind ourselves of this. Preceded by a paragraph announcing the rich promise of "the present moment" and followed by one celebrating "the sunrise and the dawn" (17), this story does not seem to belong here. Nothing prepares us for it, and it goes nowhere—except insofar as it relates to other similarly cryptic moments in *Walden.* Rather, the story surfaces inexplicably from beneath the rhetoric of morning and then retreats. Its sudden appearance in the text is as mysterious as are its elusive sources.

Like the compelling set of stories that emerges from within the trivializing frame of "Former Inhabitants," the story of the hound, bay horse, and turtledove is less important for its actual sources than for the sense of loss that it communicates.[11] In both cases, loss is feelingly evoked, given a "place," without allowing it a narrative relation to the larger development of *Walden.* The parable, discrete and enigmatic, has the effect of containing loss.

*To see *Walden* as pivotal in this sense is, perhaps, to clear up some of its ambiguities and apparent contradictions, to which critics in recent years have given great emphasis. For example, Walter Benn Michaels argues that *Walden* is a book of "false bottoms" whose textual ambiguities can "drown" us ("*Walden*'s False Bottoms," *Glyph: Johns Hopkins Textual Studies* [1977], 132–49). But, allowing for the indeterminacy of *all* literary texts, *Walden*'s bottom is firm. Its deep complexity derives from crosscurrents, such as I have described, that run at levels "above" the bottom.

This effect is analogous to the concretization of loss that we find in certain legendary objects from Walden's past: the canoe found sixty years before by an "old man" (190) who remembers, for Thoreau, a natural world of greater plenitude; or the magical chest, floating to and from the shore, reported to the same old man by another old man who lived at the Pond "before the Revolution." Like the canoe, which "belonged to the pond" (191), all such objects have a legendary association with Walden. As they merge in Thoreau's imagination with objects from his own lost youth at Walden, such as the large trunks he saw on the bottom when he "first looked into these depths" (191), they create a vision of loss that includes but transcends the personal: "Now the trunks of trees on the bottom, and the old log canoe, and the dark surrounding woods, are gone" (192).

Such examples suggest the way in which Thoreau generally treats the past in *Walden;* he treats it not historically, but mythically— through mysterious figures like the "old settler" and "elderly dame" (137) in "Solitude." Their presence evokes the sense of the Pond's deep past without ever allowing that past to become historicized. In this way, both the human past and the losses that inevitably characterize it are distanced from the particular lives and events in which they were experienced.

But by distancing loss, Thoreau also broadens its meaning. Those of whom he has inquired about his lost hound, bay horse, and turtledove "seemed as anxious to recover them as if they had lost them themselves" (17). Viewed in the light of "Former Inhabitants," this response can be understood as reciprocal. It corresponds to the "sympathy" Thoreau offers to those who, like him, have suffered time's losses. Subtly, enigmatically, *Walden*'s parables of loss—of which "Former Inhabitants" is the most sustained—extend the story of the Pond's solitary hero to include "the history of a family."

epilogue

≋

I f "the history of a family," the human family, is *Walden*'s buried
theme, we should remember that *family* is at the root of *familiar*.
Familiarization, as we saw, is one of the key processes through
which Thoreau "worlded" the world of Walden. By making Walden
familiar, he made of it a family, *his* family—a "circle of creatures" that,
for him, "complet[ed] the world." The renewal most vividly dramatized by *Walden* is the ever-recurring cycle of nature, not the linear,
historical generativity of men and women. "Former Inhabitants" shows
us that this form of generativity was a possibility whose failure in his
own life Thoreau (never marrying or fathering children) lamented, and
Walden may be regarded as pivotal in this sense as well. Taken as a
whole, it represents a choice, a commitment, to devote himself to the
family of nature; as he wrote in a Journal entry of 1857, "All nature is
my bride" (April 23, 1857: *J*, 9:337). The "book" to which he gave
himself so unreservedly in the years after *Walden*, his Journal, reflects
this choice both in its primary subject, the natural world, and in its
method. Though the Journal concerns itself with humanity and history

in many ways, its central activity, in Sharon Cameron's phrase, is writing nature.[1]

As we have seen, both *A Week* and *Walden* are recollections of past experience whose formal structures, though of different design, work toward redemption of that human experience. But the Journal is not without redemptive purpose; rather, it dramatizes this purpose in its own distinctive way. What we have here are two modes, closed and open, the former ruled by the necessities of art and performing, through art, the miracle of redemption. In the Journal, on the other hand, openness itself is redemptive, affording the largest possible space for the play of imagination. In the very act of being written, the Journal dramatizes the condition of vital engagement that Emerson called "the active soul." These differing modes of redemption suggest the ways in which the activities of writing books and of keeping a journal are forever at play with one another, shifting their balance and relation according to the pressures exerted by their respective structures.

Like *A Week* and *Walden,* the Journal keeps time through recollection, through the art of memory, but, in a way that neither of his books could do, it also keeps present time. As Thoreau writes in an entry of January 24, 1856, "The charm of the journal must consist in a certain greenness, though freshness, and not in maturity. Here I cannot afford to be remembering what I said or did, my scurf cast off, but what I am and aspire to become" (*J*, 8 : 134). That is, the Journal keeps time musically, counting out the "melodious cadences" of the present, the "consecutive sounds called a strain of music."

These are the phrases Thoreau used, on January 8, 1842, just before the onset of his brother's fatal illness, to characterize the flow of time. With the crisis of his brother's death, that music became discordant and unbearable to hear. The writing of *A Week, Walden,* and the mature Journal, each in a different way, restored for Thoreau his confidence in his relation to time and founded that relation on a new basis. The music of time with which he ultimately gained intimacy was not the "strain of music . . . wafted down through the centuries," a conception issuing from romantic sentiment, but the music of the spheres.

In this newfound, and newly founded, conception, time joined with space to form a circle, a design for the cosmos.

We have seen how Thoreau, especially in his Journal, anticipates the thought of early, objectivist modernism and even of contemporary phenomenology. But his most important relation to our time may be his engagement in the activity that Stephen Toulmin calls "[c]osmological thinking."[2] Thoreau's effort to "world" the world—to realize a cosmos—was in part a response to the confusion of his age. With the old eighteenth-century design of the universe still dominant in the religious and scientific thought of his time, he worked through the implications of romanticism to forge a new design. And for all the difficulties and contradictions inherent in his effort, it is the *activity* of his worlding that potentially serves us as an example.

Now we stand at another moment of great confusion, indeed, a moment of crisis and danger. Human intervention in natural process, as Hannah Arendt has said, began centuries ago; the capacity and the will to intervene have been with us for a long time.[3] But the effect of that intervention, in the actual living world of earth and air and water, has accelerated to massive proportions during the 130 years or so since Thoreau's death. Nature's turning wheel, in which Thoreau had such great faith (having earned it), no longer runs smoothly. His belief in an essentially stable and predictable cosmos, an eternal background for human life, is no longer possible for us.

The stunning truth of our moment is that large-scale, irreversible changes are discernibly taking place at all levels of the natural world. Indeed, the term "natural world," implying as it does nature's otherness from ourselves, begins to lose its meaning, because, increasingly, this is a world *we* have made. And our "making" is of an ominously different kind from the process through which Thoreau "made" the world of Walden. The worlding of Walden was, as we saw, a process of dilation, of opening *out*. Our worlding, in stark contrast, threatens to close the world down, if not into a "greenhouse" then into some other form of confinement.

Thoreau wrote about nature's otherness most compellingly in his great essay "Walking," published shortly after his death in 1862 but largely developed in his Journal during the early 1850s.[4] This is the essay in which he made his famous claim that "in Wildness is the preservation of the World" (*W*, 5:224). For Thoreau, this was a claim confidently, spiritedly made; it was grounded in his conviction that on "any afternoon," even in his own "vicinity," he could find "[a]n absolutely new prospect" (*W*, 5:211). "Walking" could take him to it, which is to say that the boundary between civilization and nature was both discernible and proximate. For us in the late twentieth century, it is neither. Knowing how seriously we have obscured this boundary and diminished "the wild," we also realize that we have jeopardized our "preservation." And it may be true that the only way, now, for us to assure our continuance is to develop a cosmology, to perform a "worlding," that would fundamentally alter our relation to nature.

In "Walking," Thoreau took account of his own generation's alienation from nature by observing, "We have to be told that the Greeks called the world Κόσμος, Beauty, or Order, but we do not see clearly why they did so, and we esteem it at best only a curious philological fact" (*W*, 5:242). The unawakened sense of cosmos described here is a failure of perception, a failure, literally, to "see clearly." In trying to clear the sight of his contemporaries, to bring them to their senses, Thoreau calls us to our own urgent work of perception. This is our morning work.

appendix

≈≈≈

S hown on the following pages is part of the Kalendar chart, from MA 610 in the Pierpont Morgan Library, that Thoreau titled *General Phenomena for November*. The complete chart for this month fills two double-sided sheets, both measuring 8½ by 14 inches, and the portion illustrated here (broken into two panels) is the first side, in full, of the initial sheet. The title, the headings 1852–1861, the categories of natural phenomena, and the information in the grid are written in black ink. Other, apparently tentative, notations appear in pencil.

The categories of natural phenomena shown in the illustration are

River Lowest
River Highest
Rain in First half
Rain in last half
Drizzling & misty rain
NE storm
Thunder & lightning
Rainbow

General Phenomena for November, from Thoreau's Kalendar. MA 610. The Pierpont Morgan Library, New York.

Still cloudy days
Foul in <u>AM</u>, pleasant in P<u>m</u>
Fog in morning
1st wreck line
1st really cold & wintry weather
Cold day 1st half
Cold day last half
Cold Gray Days.

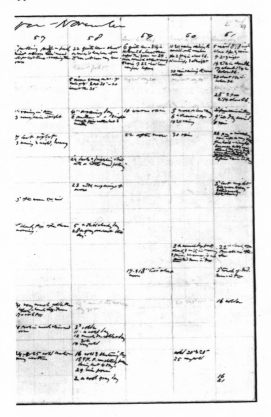

The numbers that appear within individual boxes of the grid are November dates. For example, in the box that forms the intersection of 1860 and the category "Rain in First half," Thoreau has written:

3 more or less rainy
6 a shower in P<u>m</u>
10 & 11 rainy

For another example, see the box that forms the intersection of 1853 and the category "Rainbow," where, circled and transferred to the

1852 column, appears the notation, "12 P̲m̲ a very bright rainbow." Such transferences, of which there are several in this chart, reveal the inherent difficulty of Thoreau's Kalendar-making.

Another aspect of this difficulty is shown by what may be a provisional category penciled in, probably after the full chart was drawn, just below "Still cloudy days": "Rain & clears up cold at night." This insertion (barely visible here) betrays Thoreau's desire to be comprehensive; but it also suggests a struggle to determine which natural phenomena are central and discrete enough to serve as viable categories. On subsequent pages of the November chart a number of categories, as well as information within the grid relating to them, have been crossed out.

Another feature of Thoreau's Kalendar is its mixture of objective and subjective categories. Generally the categories invite empirical observation; most of those from that portion of the November chart shown here (such as "River Lowest") are of this kind. But there are others far more subjective in character, such as the following from subsequent portions of the November chart: "Stillness which precedes winter," "End of Sauntering walks," and "Water blue as indigo."

notes

≈

PREFACE

1 Perry Miller, *Consciousness in Concord: The Text of Thoreau's Hitherto "Lost Journal" (1840–1841) Together with Notes and a Commentary* (Boston: Houghton Mifflin, 1958), 4.

2 The most fully developed study arguing this view is Sharon Cameron, *Writing Nature: Henry Thoreau's "Journal"* (New York: Oxford University Press, 1985).

CHAPTER 1. KILLING TIME

1 An example is a passage written on August 22, 1838, less than a year after Thoreau had begun his Journal: "How thrilling a noble sentiment in the oldest books—in Homer The Zendavesta—or Confucius!— It is a strain of music wafted down to us on the breeze of time, through the aisles of innumerable ages. By its very nobleness it is made near and audible to us" (*PJ*, 1:52).

2 See esp. Richard Lebeaux, *Young Man Thoreau* (Amherst: University of Massachusetts Press, 1977), 167–204.

3 In a passage titled "Crickets" from the early Journal (August 29, 1838), for example, Thoreau wonders if the sound of the crickets is "not earth herself chanting for all time" (*PJ*, 1:54).

4 Frederick Garber, *Thoreau's Redemptive Imagination* (New York: New York University Press, 1977). For further discussion of this model of Thoreau's imagination, see note on page 89.

5 In the "Historical Introduction" to the Princeton edition of *A Week,* Linck C. Johnson suggests that Thoreau changed the book's title "to stress its formal shape and de-emphasize the travel motif" (462), but, as my analysis attempts to show, the reasons lie deeper.

6 See Jack Kerouac, *Visions of Cody,* with an introduction by Allen Ginsberg (New York: McGraw-Hill, 1972), vii–xii, 103. For the importance of "recollection" in Thoreau's life as a writer, see Sherman Paul, *The Shores of America: Thoreau's Inward Exploration* (Urbana: University of Illinois Press, 1958), 192–93; and Alfred Kazin, *An American Procession* (New York: Random House, 1984), 70–71. For the river as a symbol of memory in *A Week,* see Jonathan Bishop, "The Experience of the Sacred in Thoreau's *Week,*" *ELH* 33 (1966): 76. On *A Week*'s elegiac dimension and history, see the following: John Hildebidle, *Thoreau: A Naturalist's Liberty* (Cambridge, Mass.: Harvard University Press, 1983), 8–12; Jamie Hutchinson, "'The Lapse of the Current': Thoreau's Historical Vision in *A Week on the Concord and Merrimack Rivers,*" *ESQ* 25 (1979): 212–13; Walter Hesford, "'Incessant Tragedies': A Reading of *A Week on the Concord and Merrimack Rivers,*" *ELH* 44 (1977): 519–21.

7 See Paul David Johnson, "Thoreau's Redemptive *Week,*" *American Literature* 49 (1977): 25.

8 See Lawrence Buell, *Literary Transcendentalism: Style and Vision in the American Renaissance* (Ithaca, N.Y.: Cornell University Press, 1973), 210.

9 See esp. Arendt's *Between Past and Future: Eight Exercises in Political Thought* (New York: Viking Press, 1968), 6, 285 n. 1; and *Men in Dark Times* (New York: Harcourt Brace Jovanovich, 1968), 97, 104.

10 In the paragraph following this passage, Thoreau tells that "[t]his apple-tree . . . is called 'Elisha's apple-tree,' from a friendly Indian, who was anciently in the service of Jonathan Tyng . . . [who] was killed here by his race in one of the Indian wars. . . . He was buried close by, no one knew exactly where, but in the flood of 1785, so great a weight of water standing over the grave, caused the earth to settle where it had once been disturbed, and when the flood went down, a sunken spot, exactly of the form and size of the grave, revealed its locality; but this was now lost again, and no future flood can detect it; yet, no doubt, Nature will know how to point it out in due time, if it be necessary, by methods yet more searching and unexpected" (356–57). The tree's name, thus, commemorates and "remembers" the Indians' vanished presence, but the image of Tyng's lost (dis-located) grave broadens the issue of loss to include that of white settlement as well. For an analysis of Thoreau's composition of the Jonathan Tyng passage, see Linck C. Johnson, *Thoreau's Complex Weave: The Writing of A Week on the Concord and Merrimack Rivers, With the Text of the First Draft* (Charlottesville: University Press of Virginia, 1986), 161–62.

11 Another reason is Thoreau's characteristically romantic belief in the insufficiency of language (see *Wk,* 8, 343, 391–93). For the ambiguities of his position on writing, see Eric J. Sundquist, *Home as Found: Authority and Genealogy in Nineteenth-Century American Literature* (Baltimore: Johns Hopkins University Press, 1979), 59–85; and David B. Suchoff, "'A More Conscious

Silence': Friendship and Language in Thoreau's *Week*," *ELH* 49 (1982): 673–88. Thoreau's love of oral culture is especially apparent in his Journal, where he often records stories of Concord's past told to him by local figures such as George Minnott.

12 To demote history is also to diminish the authority of society. Thoreau characteristically pits natural against human history (*Wk*, 156, 219) and the poet against the historian (*Wk*, 60, 376–77); see Hildebidle, *Naturalist's Liberty*, 7–23. See also Joan Burbick, *Thoreau's Alternative History: Changing Perspectives on Nature, Culture, and Language* (Philadelphia: University of Pennsylvania Press, 1987), for a distinction between "civil" and "uncivil" (natural) history, as this polarity is expressed in *A Week* (15–34). Since the "universal laws" reside in consciousness, Thoreau argues, "history" and "tradition" are merely "shadows of our private experiences" (*Wk*, 292; see Carl F. Hovde, "Literary Materials in Thoreau's *A Week*," *PMLA* 80 [1965]: 83).

13 See Robert F. Sayre, *Thoreau and the American Indians* (Princeton: Princeton University Press, 1977), 101–22, for a compelling and lucid exploration of this possibility. Hildebidle doubts that Thoreau had such a book in mind (70).

14 See esp. *Tristes Tropiques*, trans. John and Doreen Weightman (New York: Atheneum Press, 1974), 74.

15 Charles Olson, *The Maximus Poems*, ed. George F. Butterick (Berkeley: University of California Press, 1983), 256.

16 Thoreau spells Hannah's name "Dustan." Some recent critics read the Duston episode primarily as an *exemplum* for American violence (see Sundquist, 61–64, and Richard Slotkin, *Regeneration through Violence: The Mythology of the American Frontier, 1600–1860* [Middletown, Conn.: Wesleyan University Press, 1973], 523). Yet this view misses the quality of the narration and its relation to *A Week*'s larger purposes.

17 Among the many versions of this famous New England story, Thoreau seems to have depended primarily on Benjamin L. Mirick's *History of Haverhill, Massachusetts* (Haverhill: Thayer, 1832). For the relation of Thoreau's to Mirick's account, see Johnson, *Thoreau's Complex Weave*, 155–59. See also Robert D. Arner, "The Story of Hannah Duston: Cotton Mather to Thoreau," *American Transcendental Quarterly* 18 (1973): 19–23.

18 For *A Week*'s relation to travel literature, see John A. Christie, *Thoreau as World Traveler* (New York: Columbia University Press, 1965), 250–57.

CHAPTER 2. FURTHER DOWN THE STREAM OF TIME

1 For the river's humanizing effect on boatmen, see *Wk*, 210–11. In a Journal entry of July 2, 1858, Thoreau writes, "There is something in the scenery of a broad river equivalent to culture and civilization" (*J*, 11:4). And in an entry written almost twenty years earlier, on September 5, 1838, he records a crucial insight on the nature of rivers: "For the first time it occurred to me this afternoon what a piece of wonder a river is.—A huge volume of matter ceaselessly rolling through the fields and meadows of this substantial earth—making haste from the high places, by stable dwellings of men and Egyptian pyramids;

to its restless reservoir— One would think that, by a very natural impulse, the dwellers upon the headwaters of the Mississippi and Amazon, would follow in the trail of their waters to see the end of the matter" (*PJ*, 1:55; cf. *Wk*, 11).

2 For the seashore as "other" in *Cape Cod*, see Sherman Paul, "From Walden Out," *Thoreau Quarterly*, 16 (Winter/Spring 1984): 78. On rivers versus the sea in Thoreau, see Paul, *The Shores of America*, 201.

3 See Frederick Garber, "A Space for Saddleback: Thoreau's *A Week on the Concord and Merrimack Rivers*," *Centennial Review* 24 (1980): 327.

4 Bishop finds that in *A Week* distant objects image the sacred, whereas those near at hand image the profane (see "The Experience of the Sacred," 72–73); but as Buell points out, the book's varied and complex strategies only partially support such a generalization (*Literary Transcendentalism*, 213 n. 4).

5 Following Paul, *The Shores of America*, 191–233, numerous studies have treated the pattern of literal and spiritual discovery in *A Week*. For example, see Joyce M. Holland, "Pattern and Meaning in Thoreau's *A Week*," *Emerson Society Quarterly* 50 Supplement (1968): 48–55.

6 For Saddleback's mythic significance, see Bishop, "The Experience of the Sacred," 73–76, and William B. Stein, "Thoreau's *A Week* and *OM* Cosmography," *American Transcendental Quarterly* 11 (1971): 24–25; for discussion of it as a conjunction of Thoreau's "mystical and practical tendencies," see James McIntosh, *Thoreau as Romantic Naturalist: His Shifting Stance toward Nature* (Ithaca, N.Y.: Cornell University Press, 1974), 162. For the mythic elements in *A Week* as a whole, see Robert D. Richardson, Jr., *Myth and Literature in the American Renaissance* (Bloomington: Indiana University Press, 1978), 92–102.

7 Cf. Sayre, *Thoreau and the American Indians*, 49; Holland, "Pattern and Meaning," 53; and Hutchinson, "'The Lapse of the Current,'" 216–17, who argue that "Thursday"'s minimal description of the ascent of Agiocochook expresses a (silent) revelation because of the site's Indian identification. More convincing is Garber, who says that the episode is anticlimactic because the climb literally was uneventful, and Thoreau's fidelity to experience prevented him from exaggerating it; in this view, the writer includes the remembered Saddleback expedition in order to have a mountain ascent that can adequately symbolize what "his journey meant to him" ("A Space for Saddleback," 335–36). Cf. Buell, who finds it "saddening" that Saddleback "is not a 'real' event in *A Week*, but an analogue from the 'past' . . . , [thus] no longer accessible except to the imagination" (*Literary Transcendentalism*, 222).

8 For an important, extended discussion of this confrontation, see Garber, *Thoreau's Redemptive Imagination*, 66–128.

9 Cf. Hutchinson, for whom Thoreau's quest "is not for eternity, a life outside time, but for . . . the creative power of renewal within time" ("'The Lapse of the Current,'" 217); Hesford, who argues that in *A Week*, the "triumph [of art] eventuates through time" ("'Incessant Tragedies,'" 524); and John Carlos Rowe, *Through the Custom House: Nineteenth-Century American Fiction and Modern Poetry* (Baltimore: Johns Hopkins University Press, 1982), who says *A Week* "demonstrates how Thoreau struggles not to transcend the temporal but to enter it more authentically" (51).

10 For eloquent personal testimony on Thoreau's "lifetime work of familiarization," see Sherman Paul, "Thinking with Thoreau," *Thoreau Quarterly,* 14 (Winter 1982): 21.

11 See Johnson, who finds in "Thursday"'s change of seasons a shift from "linear" to "cyclical" time ("Thoreau's Redemptive *Week,*" 30). Cf. Hutchinson, who, committed to the view that Agiocochook represents the mythic source of time, sees the return voyage as a "lapse" into the descending course of history; the change of seasons, in this view, signals a "fall" ("'The Lapse of the Current,'" 217).

CHAPTER 3. PICTURING THE WORLD

1 For a discussion of this relation, see William Rossi, "The Journal, Self-Culture, and the Genesis of 'Walking,'" *Thoreau Quarterly* 16 (Summer/Fall 1984): 138–55.

2 Thoreau died on May 6, 1862. For brief accounts of his last days, see Walter Harding, *The Days of Henry Thoreau: A Biography* (Princeton: Princeton University Press, 1982), 464–66; and Robert D. Richardson, Jr., *Henry Thoreau: A Life of the Mind* (Berkeley: University of California Press, 1986), 388–89. The Journal's final entry, made on November 3, 1861, closes with a description of the railroad causeway following a violent storm (*J,* 14:346).

3 That was Bronson Alcott, as noted by Lawrence Buell in "Transcendentalism's Literature of the Portfolio" (paper delivered at the meeting of the Modern Language Association, New York City, December 27, 1986). For differences between Emerson's Journal and those of others in his circle, especially Alcott and Margaret Fuller, see Lawrence Rosenwald, *Emerson and the Art of the Diary* (New York: Oxford University Press, 1988), 83–98.

4 See William Howarth, "Successor to *Walden?* Thoreau's 'Moonlight—An Intended Course of Lectures,'" *Proof 2* (1972): 92–93; Rossi, "The Journal, Self-Culture, and 'Walking,'" 141; and "Historical Introduction," *PJ,* 3:483–84 and passim.

5 Miller, *Consciousness in Concord,* 4.

6 Ibid., 31. For a recent discussion of the development of Thoreau's career in relation to the literary marketplace, see Michael T. Gilmore, *American Romanticism and the Marketplace* (Chicago: University of Chicago Press, 1985), 35–51.

7 For example, the findings of Cameron's *Writing Nature,* for all the considerable light they shed on the Journal's significance, are skewed by her general acceptance of Miller's compensation theory. The result, I think, is an exaggeration of the formal differences between *Walden* and the Journal, and a neglect of the Journal's later volumes.

8 Paul, in *The Shores of America.*

9 For example, there is widely expressed in the Journal of the early 1850s a strong, Wordsworthian desire to repossess childhood experience. On July 16, 1851, Thoreau writes: "In youth before I lost any of my senses—I can remember that I was all alive—and inhabited my body with inexpressible satisfac-

tion" (*PJ*, 3:305–6). This was the period during which Thoreau felt most fully
the impact of European romanticism. See Stephen Adams and Donald Ross,
Jr., on his "conversion to romanticism," *Revising Mythologies: The Composition of Thoreau's Major Works* (Charlottesville: University Press of Virginia,
1988), 155–64. Cf. McIntosh, *Thoreau as Romantic Naturalist,* pp. 50–51 and
passim.

10 Robert Sattelmeyer, "'Reporter to a Journal, of No Very Wide Circulation':
The Literary Career of Henry Thoreau" (paper delivered at the meeting of the
Modern Language Association, New York City, December 27, 1986). See also
"Historical Introduction," *PJ*, 3:489.

11 Sherman Paul writes: "The *Journal* was thus a kind of memory, in which
thoughts were hived against the time when, as Emerson said, these golden
boughs joined hands" ("A Note on the Composition of *Walden*," in *Walden
and Civil Disobedience,* ed. Sherman Paul [Boston: Houghton Mifflin, 1957],
xli).

12 See *W*, 5:130. This idea was first expressed in Thoreau's Journal in an entry
made on December 16, 1837: "The fact will one day flower out into a truth"
(*PJ*, 1:19).

13 For example, in an entry made soon after Thoreau began to keep his Journal,
he writes, "As a child looks forward to the coming of the summer—so could
we contemplate with quiet joy the circle of the seasons returning without fail
eternally" (January 6, 1838: *PJ*, 1:25). Two and a half years later, in an entry of
June 17, 1840, he celebrates the process of "revolving incessantly through all
circles . . . [and thus] acquir[ing] a perfect sphericity" (*PJ*, 1:130); for similar
images of sphericity written in the same period, see the first section of "The
Service" (*RP*, 3–8). See also Thoreau's early essay, "The Seasons" (1828–29;
EEM, 3) and his review of William Howitt's *The Book of the Seasons; or The
Calendar of Nature* (1836; *EEM*, 26–36).

14 *Emerson and Literary Change* (Cambridge, Mass.: Harvard University Press,
1978), 134–59. Thoreau's "circle of time" Journal passage has received surprisingly little attention. Richardson mentions it in passing, without quoting it and
without providing interpretative commentary (*Henry Thoreau,* 271). Burbick
quotes a phrase from it, glossing it in this way: "The succession of time, if
properly recorded, displayed a continual return to promise" (*Thoreau's Alternative History,* 13). Those who have come closest to seeing the passage's significance are Adams and Ross, who comment: "Presumably he [Thoreau] discovered for the first time in 1852 the psychological and mythical importance of
spring for himself and his book [*Walden*]" (*Revising Mythologies,* 168). But
here, too, no attention is given to the specifically and poignantly *visual* aspect
of this discovery.

15 William Butler Yeats, *A Vision* (New York: Macmillan, 1937), 65–184. Also
see Wendell Berry's poem, "The Wheel," in Berry's collection of the same title
([San Francisco: North Point, 1982], 48), where time and timelessness are
joined in this image. The epigraph that Berry chose for this collection, from
the writings of Sir Albert Howard, is also relevant: "It needs a more refined

perception to recognize throughout this stupendous wealth of varying shapes and forms the principle of stability. Yet this principle dominates. It dominates by means of an ever-recurring cycle . . . repeating itself silently and cease-lessly. . . . An eastern religion calls this cycle the Wheel of Life and no better name could be given to it. The revolutions of this Wheel never falter and are perfect."

16 The term "Kalendar" derives from Sherman Paul, *The Shores of America,* who uses it to describe a larger, incomplete project that would have included the charts as well as other materials, such as the late essay "Autumnal Tints" and a planned work called "November Lights." In Paul's view, this larger project would have been "a study of the entire economy of nature" (399–400), a view generally supported recently by Richardson, *Henry Thoreau* (271, 381–82). Hildebidle doubts that this was Thoreau's goal for these materials (*Natural-ists's Liberty,* 70). My own use of the term "Kalendar" applies specifically to the charts described in this chapter. The form of these charts derives from eighteenth- and early nineteenth-century models—Gilbert White's *Garden Kalendar* (1751–68), for example—whose observations of phenomena had been recorded in this way. For a discussion of White and Thoreau, see Donald Worster, *Nature's Economy: A History of Ecological Ideas* (Cambridge: Cam-bridge University Press, 1977), 2–111; and Hildebidle, 24–39, 71–73, and pas-sim. For Thoreau's interest in phenology (the study of seasonal change) as ex-pressed in the late Journal and other of his late writings, see William Howarth, *The Book of Concord: Thoreau's Life as a Writer* (New York: Penguin Books, 1982), 162–89.

17 Frances Yates, *The Art of Memory* (Chicago: University of Chicago Press, 1966), esp. 1–198.

18 Rudolf Arnheim, "Space as an Image of Time," in *Images of Romanticism: Ver-bal and Visual Affinities* (New Haven: Yale University Press, 1978), 1, 3.

19 Cf. Emerson, in his essay "Memory": "The memory has a fine art of sifting out the pain and keeping all the joy" (*Natural History of Intellect and Other Papers* [Cambridge, Mass.: Riverside Press, 1904], 104).

20 Thoreau first mentions Gilpin in his Journal in an entry of March 31, 1852, where he reflects upon the importance of Gilpin's work (having recently read Gilpin's *Remarks on Forest Scenery and Other Woodland Views, Relative Chiefly to Picturesque Beauty Illustrated by the Scenes of New Forest, in Hamp-shire. . . . ,* 3d ed. [London: T. Cadell & W. Davies, 1808]). After citing Gilpin's classification of copses and glens, he writes: "It would be worth the while to tell why a swamp pleases us.— what kinds please us—also what weather &c &c analyse our impressions. Why the moaning of the storm gives me pleasure" (*J,* 3:366). Thoreau was also influenced, but to a lesser extent, by Uvedale Price, on whose *Essays on the Picturesque, as Compared with the Sub-lime and the Beautiful; and on the Use of Studying Pictures, for the Purpose of Improving Real Landscape,* 3 vols. (London: J. Mawman, 1810) he comments in a Journal entry of February 6, 1854 (*J,* 6:103).

21 Emerson's own Journal, with its more diverse agenda, is far less given to land-

scape description than is Thoreau's. For a consideration of that agenda, see Rosenwald, *Emerson and the Art of the Diary.* See also Joel Porte's preface and his introductory commentaries in *Emerson in His Journals,* ed. Joel Porte (London: Cambridge University Press, 1982). For a detailed examination of Thoreau's "optics," see Richard J. Schneider, "Reflections in Walden Pond: Thoreau's Optics," *ESQ* 21 (2d Quarter 1975): 65–81.

22 The lily as an emblem of purity also appears in the conclusion of "Slavery in Massachusetts" (*RP,* 108–9). For a discussion of its significance in that essay, see McIntosh, *Thoreau as Romantic Naturalist,* 29–30; and Lawrence Buell, "American Pastoral Ideology Reappraised," *American Literary History* 1 (Spring 1989): 6–7.

23 See Ethel Seybold, *Thoreau: The Quest and the Classics* (New Haven: Yale University Press, 1951), 80, on how Thoreau "could not help from speculating" on the symbolic meaning of such natural objects.

24 See esp. Barbara Novak, *American Painting of the Nineteenth Century* (New York: Praeger Publishers, 1969); and Novak, *Nature and Culture: American Landscape Painting, 1825–1875* (New York: Oxford University Press, 1980).

25 For an important reconsideration of the relation between Puritan figural understandings of nature and the symbolism of nineteenth-century American romanticism, see Sacvan Bercovitch, *The Puritan Origins of the American Self* (New Haven: Yale University Press, 1975), 136–86; see also Bercovitch, *The American Jeremiad* (Madison: University of Wisconsin Press, 1978).

26 As often observed, Emerson's notions of the symbolic relation of language and nature came to him, in part, from Emanuel Swedenborg and Sampson Reed. For a particularly cogent explanation of this influence, see Philip F. Gura, *The Wisdom of Words: Language, Theology, and Literature in the New England Renaissance* (Middletown, Conn.: Wesleyan University Press, 1981), chap. 3; for Thoreau's own distinctive adaptation of these ideas, see Gura, chap. 4. See John Irwin, *American Hieroglyphics: The Symbol of the Egyptian Hieroglyphics in the American Renaissance* (New Haven: Yale University Press, 1980), for the way in which Champollion's decoding of the hieroglyphics intensified the search for nature's symbolic meaning among mid-nineteenth-century American romantic writers, including Thoreau. On the American nineteenth-century symbolic imagination, see Charles Feidelson, Jr., *Symbolism and American Literature* (Chicago: University of Chicago Press, 1953).

27 Cf. McIntosh on Thoreau as a "beleaguered symbolist . . . , doing his best to be faithful to both fact and value" (*Thoreau as Romantic Naturalist,* 35). See also Cameron, who argues that in his Journal Thoreau found a "nature that resists being symbolic" (*Writing Nature,* 61) and that in the act of "writing nature" Emersonian correspondence broke down for him.

28 Sherman Paul, *Emerson's Angle of Vision: Man and Nature in American Experience* (Cambridge, Mass.: Harvard University Press, 1952), 80–87.

29 See Paul's distinction, derived from José Ortega y Gasset, between Emerson's "proximate vision" and "distant vision," in *Emerson's Angle of Vision,* 75–79.

30 Discussions of Thoreau's relation to luminism include Barton Levi St. Armand,

"Luminism in the Work of Henry David Thoreau: The Dark and the Light," *Canadian Review of American Studies* 11 (Spring 1980): 13–30; John Conron, "Bright American Rivers: The Luminist Landscapes of Thoreau's *A Week on the Concord and Merrimack Rivers*," *American Quarterly* 32 (1980): 143–66; Richard J. Schneider, "Thoreau and Nineteenth-Century American Landscape Painting," *ESQ*, 31 (1985); 67–88; Kevin Radaker, "'A Separate Intention of the Eye': Luminist Eternity in Thoreau's *A Week on the Concord and Merrimack Rivers*," *Canadian Review of American Studies* 18 (1987): 41–60. For a useful, brief summary of Thoreau's attitudes toward the visual arts, see Edward Wagenknecht, *Henry David Thoreau: What Manner of Man?* (Amherst: University of Massachusetts Press, 1981), 32–34. Gayle L. Smith, in "Emerson and the Luminist Painters: A Study of Their Styles," *American Quarterly* 37: 193–215, finds Emerson's vision "horizontal" and luminist, not in his landscape description, but in the paratactic structure of his sentences.

31 See esp. Novak's two works, cited in n. 24. On the importance of vision and optics in Emerson, see F. O. Matthiessen, *American Renaissance: Art and Expression in the Age of Emerson and Whitman* (New York: Oxford University Press, 1941), xiv; Sherman Paul, *Emerson's Angle of Vision;* and Barbara Packer, *Emerson's Fall: A New Interpretation of the Major Essays* (New York: Continuum, 1982), 73–77.

32 Lisa Fellows Andrus describes the way in which Lane "maintained the topographer's allegiance to the accuracy of the view but, through the principles of art, elevated the factual to the poetic." His "commitment to the carefully measured view," Andrus continues, "is documented by the ruled grid superimposed over the drawing to aid in the transfer of the scene to the canvas" ("Design and Measurement in Luminist Art," in *American Light: The Luminist Movement 1850–1875*, ed. John Wilmerding (New York: Harper & Row, in association with the National Gallery of Art, 1980), 40.

33 The immediate impetus for Thoreau's interest in analogy, as expressed in this passage, was his interest in James John Garth Wilkinson's scholarly probes into the origins of words, in Wilkinson's *The Human Body and Its Connection with Man, Illustrated by the Principal Organs* (Philadelphia: Lippincott & Grambo, 1851).

34 Laurence Stapleton, "Introduction," in *H. D. Thoreau: A Writer's Journal*, ed. Laurence Stapleton (New York: Dover, 1960), xv–xvi. See also Stapleton's chapter on Thoreau in her *The Elected Circle: Studies in the Art of Prose* (Princeton: Princeton University Press, 1973), 195–232. Cf. Schneider: "[I]n addition to the Emersonian theory of symbolic correspondence between natural fact and spiritual truth, Thoreau was interested in what might be called 'co-respondence,' the mutual and active response of man to nature and of nature to man" ("Reflections in Walden Pond," 68).

35 Nina Baym, "Thoreau's View of Science," *Journal of the History of Ideas*, 26 (1965): esp. 233–34. For a recent discussion of Thoreau's complex attitudes toward the relation of science and art, as they may have been influenced by the thought of Samuel Taylor Coleridge, see Robert Sattelmeyer and Richard A.

Hocks, "Thoreau and Coleridge's *Theory of Life,*" *Studies in the American Renaissance: 1985,* ed. Joel Myerson (Charlottesville: University Press of Virginia, 1985), 269–84.

36 See esp. Hildebidle, *Naturalist's Liberty,* chaps. 2, 3, and 5; Robert Sattelmeyer, "Introduction," *Henry David Thoreau: The Natural History Essays* (Salt Lake City: Peregrine Smith, 1984), xxv–xxvi; and Worster, *Nature's Economy,* chaps. 3 and 4.

Even when Thoreau is contrasting the scientist and the poet, the comparison is not always invidious. On November 8, 1858, he writes in his Journal: "Lichen as they affect the scenery, as picturesque objects described by Gilpin or others, are one thing; as they concern the lichenist, quite another" (*J,* 11:297). Yet, his emphasis here is on the scientist's admirably acute powers of observation, as an earlier passage from the same entry shows: "It is remarkable how little any but a lichenist will observe on the bark of trees. The mass of men have but the vaguest and most indefinite notion of mosses. . . . They see bark as if they saw it not" (*J,* 11:296). Not only did Thoreau value the work of the scientist; in nineteenth-century terms, he *was* one—a capable botanist, for one thing. See Ray Angelo, "Thoreau as Botanist," *Thoreau Quarterly* 15 (1983): 15–31, and Angelo's "Botanical Index to the Journal of Henry David Thoreau" in the same volume, 39–201.

37 In certain respects, Thoreau's negative reaction to Ruskin was not uncharacteristic of American thinkers at mid-century. See Roger B. Stein, *John Ruskin and Aesthetic Thought in America, 1840–1900* (Cambridge, Mass.: Harvard University Press, 1967), esp. 90–94. For two other damaging assessments of Ruskin's work by Thoreau, one implicit and the other explicit, see *J,* 10:80 and *J,* 10:147. In generally recommending Ruskin's books to H. G. O. Blake, in a letter of November 16, 1857, Thoreau nevertheless found them "not without crudeness and bigotry" (*C,* 497).

38 As Robert Sattelmeyer points out, Thoreau's Harvard studies instructed him in philosophical idealism, which was reinforced in the early 1840s by his reading of such authors as Ralph Cudworth, Joseph Marie de Gérando, and François de Salignac de la Mothe Fénelon (*Thoreau's Reading: A Study in Intellectual History, with Bibliographical Catalogue* [Princeton: Princeton University Press, 1988], 28).

39 Concerning this issue, McIntosh writes: "Nature is for [Thoreau] a powerful and mysterious independent realm, not a mere projection of himself. Yet it is inarticulate. It is of no use to him or to the human community until he perceives and describes it. This is a naturalistic version of Emersonian idealism" (*Thoreau as Romantic Naturalist,* 36). See also Schneider, who says that "ultimately [Thoreau] attempted to steer a middle course between" idealism and empiricism ("Reflections in Walden Pond," 65).

40 William James, "A World of Pure Experience," in *Essays in Radical Empiricism* (Cambridge, Mass.: Harvard University Press, 1976; first published, posthumously, in 1912), 22.

41 Fenollosa's essay was first published in *Little Magazine* in 1919, and is reprinted in Karl Shapiro, ed., *Prose Keys to Modern Poetry* (Evanston, Ill.: Row,

Peterson, 1962), in which the quoted passages appear on p. 148. Pound distinguishes between "true" and "untrue" metaphor in his "Prolegomena." For Schneidau's illuminating discussion of Fenollosa's influence on Pound, see his *Ezra Pound: The Image and the Real* (Baton Rouge: Louisiana State University Press, 1969), 56–73.

42 These imperatives were stated by F. S. Flint in the second issue of Harriet Monroe's magazine, *Poetry,* in March 1913.

43 Stephen Owen, *Traditional Chinese Poetry and Poetics: Omen of the World* (Madison: University of Wisconsin Press, 1985), 57. Owen's subtitle suggests the process I call "worldling," in my discussion of *Walden* in chap. 5.

44 Stephen Owen, *Remembrances: The Experience of the Past in Classical Chinese Literature* (Cambridge, Mass.: Harvard University Press, 1986), 139.

45 Owen, *Traditional Chinese Poetry and Poetics,* 96, 100.

46 For example, see Thoreau's extended treatment of the cranberry and huckleberry in a Journal entry of August 30, 1856 (*J,* 9:35–46).

47 Gaston Bachelard, *The Poetics of Reverie: Childhood, Language, and the Cosmos,* trans. Daniel Russell (Boston: Beacon Press, 1969).

48 See Sherman Paul, "The Husbandry of the Wild," *Iowa Review* 17 (Spring/Summer 1987): 12, on the relation of phenology to phenomenology in the works of Aldo Leopold.

CHAPTER 4. THE CATEGORICAL IMAGINATION

1 Jakobson linked metonymy to a form of aphasia in which the patient is capable of predicating the perceived object but incapable of naming it. The relevant essay is "Two Aspects of Language and Two Types of Aphasic Disturbances," in Roman Jakobson, *Fundamentals of Language,* with Morris Halle (The Hague: Mouton, 1971), 69–96.

2 Thoreau delivered his address "The Succession of Forest Trees" to the Middlesex Agricultural Society in Concord in September 1860; see *Excursions* (*W,* 9:184–204). His identification of a new species of bream in Walden Pond occurred during November 1858. On November 26, describing his examination of some minnows, he says: "[F]rom their form and single dorsal fin, I think they are breams. Are they not a new species?" (*J,* 11:347). The imaginative dimension of this discovery is suggested in an entry of four days later: "When my eyes first rested on Walden the striped bream was poised in it, though I did not see it, and when Tahatawan paddled his canoe there. How wild it makes the pond and the township to find a new fish in it! America renews her youth here" (*J,* 11:358).

3 For example, in a Journal entry of February 7, 1858, Thoreau gives instructions on how to gain aesthetic advantage from the "distant" view: "If possible, come upon the top of a hill unexpectedly, perhaps through woods, and then see off from it to the distant earth which lies behind a bluer veil, before you can see directly down it, *i.e.* bringing its own near top against the distant landscape" (*J,* 10:276).

4 Thomas S. Kuhn, *The Structure of Scientific Revolutions,* 2d ed. (Chicago: Uni-

versity of Chicago Press, 1970), chap. 5; Michael Polanyi, *The Tacit Dimension* (Garden City, N.Y.: Doubleday), 1966.

5 See esp. Gombrich's *Art and Illusion: A Study in the Psychology of Pictorial Representation,* 4th ed. (Princeton: Princeton University Press, 1972).

6 Cf. Burbick, who writes of Thoreau's "new precision [around 1845] in viewing space within a cartographical grid [whereby] a unit of time is wedded to a recognition of the illusory quality of seeing," leading to "a style of description in the *Journal* that balances the stability of spatial grids with the fleeting effects of time" (*Thoreau's Alternative History,* 40).

7 See *On Poetic Imagination and Reverie: Selections from the Works of Gaston Bachelard,* trans. Colette Gaudin (Indianapolis: Bobbs-Merrill, 1971), 84–88.

8 The passage describing "the reign of water" cited earlier in this chapter was from the fall of 1857, but three and a half years before this, in the spring of 1854, Thoreau had observed, "Now is the reign of water" (March 12, 1854: *J,* 6:166).

9 This statement, which I take to be entirely sincere, directly contradicts Miller's claim that Thoreau, like many another New Englander, dreaded winter ("winter killed him") and lived only for spring (*Consciousness in Concord,* 104–5).

10 The phrase "first facts" belongs to Lawrence Willson, who uses it in referring to Thoreau's deep interest in originating moments in nature and history: "The Influence of Early North American History and Legend on the Writing of Henry David Thoreau" (Ph.D. diss., Yale University, 1949), 119–60 and passim.

11 For examples of this question, see *J,* 10:447 (1858); *J,* 12:387–88 (1859); and *J,* 13:425–26 (1860). For its relevance to Thoreau's scientific pursuits, see Baym, "Thoreau's View of Science," 226–27.

12 This Pythagorean figure appears early in Thoreau's writings; see, for example, his Journal entries on "sphere music" written on August 5 and September 2, 1838 (*PJ,* 1:50, 54–55), and the section of his early essay "The Service" called "What Music Shall We Have?" (*RP,* 9–12). For a discussion of the sources of Thoreau's "metaphysics of sound," see Paul, *The Shores of America,* 64–67 and passim.

13 Edward Said, *Beginnings: Intention and Method* (New York: Basic Books, 1975), esp. chap. 1; Frank Kermode, *The Sense of an Ending: Studies in the Theory of Fiction* (London: Oxford University Press, 1966), esp. chap. 2.

14 Alfred North Whitehead, *Science and the Modern World: Lowell Lectures, 1925* (New York: Macmillan, 1925), 95.

15 Ibid., 121. See also Whitehead's *Process and Reality: An Essay in Cosmology* (New York: Macmillan, 1929), esp. pt. 2.

16 See esp. Edmund Burke, *A Philosophical Enquiry into the Origin of Our Ideas of the Sublime and Beautiful,* ed. James T. Boulton (Notre Dame, Ind.: University of Notre Dame Press, 1958; first published, 1757): "*[S]moothness* is a principal cause of pleasure to the touch, taste, smell, and hearing, [and] it will be easily admitted a constituent of visual beauty"; "[t]here can be no doubt that

bodies which are rough and angular, rouse and vellicate the organs of feeling, causing a sense of pain" (151).

17 To see this dream as dramatizing the process of individuation is to understand it more from a Lacanian than a Freudian point of view. See esp. Jacques Lacan, "The Mirror Stage as Formative of the Function of the I as Revealed in Psychoanalytic Experience," in *Écrits: A Selection,* trans. Alan Sheridan (London: Tavistock, 1977), 1–7. For a Freudian interpretation of the passage, see Richard Lebeaux, for whom this dream reveals "sexual and oedipal connotations, the cycle of pleasure and fatal punishment," and evidence of Thoreau's "frequent swings of mood and perception" (*Thoreau's Seasons* [Amherst: University of Massachusetts Press, 1984], 250).

18 In comparing *Walden* to *Cape Cod,* Sherman Paul speaks of the way in which *Walden* dramatizes "the familiarization by which [the Pond] becomes place and answers to the deepest necessities of self" ("From Walden Out," 74).

19 Empson defines "the pastoral process" as one of "putting the complex into the simple," in his *Some Versions of Pastoral* (New York: New Directions, 1950), 22. See also Herbert Lindenberger, "The Idyllic Moment: On Pastoral and Romanticism," *College English* 34 (December 1972): 335–51. A discussion of Cooper's Glimmerglass as a pastoral setting appears in my *A World by Itself: The Pastoral Moment in Cooper's Fiction* (New Haven: Yale University Press, 1977), 184–85 and passim; see pp. 10–13 of this work for differences between Cooper's Glimmerglass and Thoreau's Walden. John Seelye compares the pastoralism of Cooper and Thoreau in "Some Green Thoughts on a Green Theme," *TriQuarterly* no. 23/24 (Winter-Spring 1972): 576–638.

20 For example, Paul views the Pond's "stony shore" as a symbol of Thoreau's "empirical self, the self he wanted to purify" (*The Shores of America,* 333).

21 For an illustration of the measured pencil sketch that Lane drew in preparation for this painting, see Andrus, "Design and Measurement in Luminist Art," 41.

22 After the publication of *A Week* in 1849, Thoreau did only limited work on *Walden* until early 1852, when he returned to it with renewed vigor and a set of new emphases. As J. Lyndon Shanley demonstrates, his revisions during the period from 1852 to 1854 included marking with greater clarity "the full turn of the seasons" (*The Making of Walden, with the Text of the First Version* [Chicago: University of Chicago Press, 1957], 30–31, 91). See also Adams and Ross, *Revising Mythologies,* 166ff; and "Historical Introduction," *PJ,* 3:483 and passim.

CHAPTER 5. THE WORLDING OF WALDEN

1 As Charles R. Anderson, considering the loon passage as a reworking of an Algonquin myth, points out, Thoreau gives the loon a wildness "entirely missing from the Indian legends" and gave even greater emphasis to this quality in the first version of "Brute Neighbors" (*The Magic Circle of Walden* [New York: Holt, Rinehart, and Winston, 1968], 196–97). This great passage, as well

as the passage that begins "Why do these objects which we behold make a world?", are late additions to *Walden*—both indebted to Thoreau's rich discoveries of perception in the early 1850s. See Shanley, *The Making of Walden,* 72–73, and Adams and Ross, *Revising Mythologies,* 169–70.

2 Suzanne Langer, *Problems of Art: Ten Philosophical Lectures* (New York: Charles Scribner's Sons, 1957), 10.

3 José Ortega y Gasset, *Meditations on Hunting,* trans. Howard B. Wescott (New York: Charles Scribner's Sons, 1972), 87.

4 Ibid., 150, 141, 142. For a consideration of "alertness [as] a way of being in the world" in Thoreau's work, especially as this relates to English romantic poets such as Wordsworth, see Frederick Garber, "Thoreau's Ladder of Alertness," *Thoreau Quarterly* 14 (Summer/Fall 1982): 118.

5 Henry G. Bugbee, Jr., *The Inward Morning: A Philosophical Exploration in Journal Form* (State College, Pa.: Bald Eagle Press, 1958), 52.

6 Ibid.

7 Richard Pevear, "Poetry and Worldlessness," *Hudson Review* 29 (Summer 1976): 318, 315, 319.

8 The most comprehensive treatment of Thoreau's relevance to twentieth-century political and social issues is to be found in Michael Meyer, *Several More Lives to Live: Thoreau's Political Reputation in America* (Westport, Conn.: Greenwood Press, 1977).

9 Maurice Merleau-Ponty, "The Primacy of Perception and Its Philosophical Consequences," trans. James M. Edie, in Merleau-Ponty's *The Primacy of Perception and Other Essays on Phenomenological Psychology, the Philosophy of Art, History and Politics,* ed. James M. Edie (Evanston, Ill.: Northwestern University Press, 1964), 16.

10 Isaac Rosenfeld, "The Meaning of Terror," in *An Age of Enormity: Life and Writing in the Forties and Fifties,* ed. Theodore Solotaroff (Cleveland: World Publishing Co., 1962), 206–9; Olson, *The Maximus Poems,* 584.

11 Cf. "A Winter Walk," where Thoreau writes: "In summer it [the Pond] is the earth's liquid eye; a mirror in the breast of nature" (*W,* 5:174); and *PJ,* 1:198, from which this ("Winter Walk") passage derives. See also Emerson in *Nature:* "The ruin or the blank, that we see when we look at nature, is in our own eye. The axis of vision is not coincident with the axis of things, and so they appear not transparent but opake" (*CW,* 1:43).

12 Martin Heidegger, "Building Dwelling Thinking," in *Poetry, Language, Thought,* trans. Albert Hofstadter (New York: Harper, Row, 1971), 145, 146, 149. Cf. Burbick, who writes: "[U]nlike Heidegger, Thoreau has an empirical need to assert a particular geographical site, which leads him to a pragmatic consideration of space" (*Thoreau's Alternative History,* 61). But as my discussion indicates, Heidegger's notion of dwelling implicitly contains—indeed, necessitates—"a particular geographical site." And, in any case, Thoreau's relation to Walden is "pragmatic" only in part.

13 Cf. Lewis H. Miller, Jr., who argues that "Thoreau's most effective writing relies on a paradoxical tension arising from his secure awareness of limits," and

that the artistic success of *Walden* depends on its being "a world bounded for the sake of boundlessness." Miller's counterpoint is *The Maine Woods,* where, he says, Thoreau "confronts a limitless wilderness which defies precise measurement and exact determination of boundaries, [and, as a result,] the elasticity of his imagination atrophies and his writing suffers" ("The Artist as Surveyor in *Walden* and *The Maine Woods, ESQ* 21 [2d quarter 1975]: 76, 77). See also Schneider, who writes, "After exploring the extremes of his world, [Thoreau] felt that it was crucial to return always to a balanced middle position" ("Reflections in Walden Pond," 68).

14 Heidegger, "Building Dwelling Thinking," 154.

15 Ibid., 156. What Heidegger calls "space as *extensio*" (155) might, from a mythological perspective such as that of Mircea Eliade, be called "sacred." For a compelling reading of *Walden* from this perspective, see David E. Whisnant, "The Sacred and the Profane in *Walden,*" *Centennial Review* 14 (Summer 1970): 267–83.

16 Cf. Emerson in *Nature:* "A work of art is an abstract or epitome of the world" (*CW,* 1:16).

17 As chapter 6 will make clear, I do not mean this quite in the same sense as Leo Marx does when he says that in *Walden,* Thoreau "removes [the pastoral hope] from history, where it is manifestly unrealizable, and relocates it in literature [its traditional location]" (*The Machine in the Garden: Technology and the Pastoral Ideal in America* [New York: Oxford University Press, 1964], 265). In *Walden,* Thoreau is never so definitive as this, never completely removes his pastoral vision from history. This vision is "literary," to be sure, but literary rather in the same sense that Paul and Percival Goodman's alternative models of community are—imaginable, in some sense even realizable, human worlds. See their *Communitas: Means of Livelihood and Ways of Life* (New York: Random House, 1947), esp. chap. 1. Thoreau's pastoral is, we may say, creative and visionary in its exploration ("visioning") of the possibilities of the future, both for the self and, by implication, for society. For a challenging reconsideration of Thoreau's relation to American pastoralism, and of American pastoralism itself, see Buell, "American Pastoral Ideology Reappraised."

CHAPTER 6. CONJURING THE PAST

1 Cf. Thoreau's essay "Wild Apples," (*W,* 9:290–322).

2 See Paul, who says of "Former Inhabitants; and Winter Visitors": "It was the time of thought and memory, of his communion with the former inhabitants of the pond whose lives introduced the possibility of failure" (*The Shores of America,* 341).

3 This image of the conviviality of an inn is prefigured in Thoreau's early essay, "The Landlord" (*W,* 5:153–62).

4 Cf. Lawrence Buell, *New England Literary Culture: From Revolution Through Renaissance* (Cambridge: Cambridge University Press, 1986), who writes of the setting of "Former Inhabitants": "[Thoreau] probably does not realize that the

ghost town, as an act of private fantasy, might serve as a monitory image of
the social consequences of willful individualism, which might not be able to
replace the literal Concord (spectral as he is pleased to regard it) with anything
more substantial than another abandoned cabin. On the contrary, the inmost
layer of the ruminations here seems not to be this ironic self-consciousness but
the intensity of the speaker's continuing desire—partly concealed from himself
through the air of playful sketchery—to rebuild town society on his own
terms" (333). But, as I have tried to show, one needn't choose an "inmost
layer." Both individual and community, both pastoral and social visions, exist
in *Walden* in a dialectical relationship.

5 As the title of her book suggests, Mary Elkins Moller gives emphasis to
Thoreau's concern for "community": *Thoreau in the Human Community*
(Amherst: University of Massachusetts Press, 1980). See esp. her discussion of
Thoreau's "gone to seed country" (145–53). Such a view of Thoreau is strenu-
ously resisted by the following, each of whom emphasizes the writer's mis-
anthropy: Leon Edel, "Henry D. Thoreau," in *Six Classic American Writers:
An Introduction,* ed. Sherman Paul (Minneapolis: University of Minnesota
Press, 1970), 160–94; Richard Bridgman, *Dark Thoreau* (Lincoln: University
of Nebraska Press, 1982); and Miller, *Consciousness in Concord.*

6 Thoreau's skill at, and pleasure in, storytelling shows up in many places in the
Journal. As William Howarth points out, one of the Journal's best (and funniest)
stories concerns the escape and recapture of a pig belonging to Thoreau's
father (August 8, 1856: *J,* 8:451–56; Howarth, *The Book of Concord,* 124–25).

7 Charles Olson, *Archaeologist of Morning* (London: Cape Goliard Press, in association with Grossman, 1970).

8 For a paragraph-by-paragraph designation of the elements of "Former Inhabitants" according to the versions of the *Walden* manuscript in which they first
appeared, see Ronald Earl Clapper, "The Development of *Walden:* A Genetic
Text" (Ph.D. diss., University of California, Los Angeles, 1967), 677–714. Also
see Shanley, *The Making of Walden,* 72–73.

9 Paul, *The Shores of America,* 292.

10 Modern scholars have shown us just how contemporaneous the composition
of these two works was. During the mid-1840s, *Walden* "proceeded in parallel
with [*A Week*]" (Sattelmeyer, *PJ,* 2:457), and Thoreau "was preparing to make
a fair copy of *Walden*" even before the publication of *A Week* (Johnson,
Thoreau's Complex Weave, 245). To consider the two books in this way is to
emphasize just how much they are companion works, dramatizing two sides of
the same life, examining in different ways the same set of experiences. To be
sure, *Walden* reflects the great intellectual discoveries recorded in the Journal
of the early 1850s; it especially shows Thoreau's confidence in the natural cycle
that his discovery of the circle of time in 1852 inspired. But the many striking
differences between these works are due not so much to the lapse of time between their moments of publication as to the thematic emphases that Thoreau
intended for each of them, and to the demands of their respective structures.

11 See Stanley Cavell (*The Senses of Walden* [New York: Viking Press, 1972]), who writes of the hound, bay horse, and turtledove passage: "The writer comes to us from a sense of loss; the myth does not contain more than symbols because it is no set of desired things he has lost, but a connection with things, the track of desire itself" (50). See also Barbara Johnson, *A World of Difference* (Baltimore: Johns Hopkins University Press, 1987): "*Walden*'s great achievement is to wake us up to our own losses, to make us participate in the trans-individual movement of loss in its infinite particularity, urging us passionately to follow the tracks of we know not quite what, as if we had lost it, or were in danger of losing it, ourselves.

"In order to communicate the irreducibly particular yet ultimately unreadable nature of loss, Thoreau has chosen to use three symbols [the hound, bay horse, and turtledove] that clearly *are* symbols but that do not really symbolize anything outside themselves" (53). As Johnson points out, Thoreau provides his own commentary on this passage in a letter to B. B. Wiley, written April 26, 1857: "How shall we account for our pursuits if they are original? We get the language with which to describe our various lives out of a common mint. If others have their losses, which they are busy repairing, so have I *mine,* & their hound & horse may *perhaps* be the symbols of some of them. But also I have lost, or am in danger of losing, a far finer & more etherial treasure, which commonly no loss of which they are conscious will symbolize—this I answer hastily & with some hesitation, according as I now understand my own words" (*C,* 478).

EPILOGUE

1 Cameron, *Writing Nature.*
2 Stephen Toulmin, *The Return to Cosmology: Postmodern Science and the Theology of Nature* (Berkeley: University of California Press, 1982), 226.
3 See Arendt, *The Human Condition* (Chicago: University of Chicago Press, 1958), esp. chap. 6.
4 For the relation of "Walking" to the Journal of this period, see Rossi, "The Journal, Self-Culture, and the Genesis of 'Walking,'" 142–43. The otherness of nature celebrated in "Walking" is different from the starkly inhuman landscapes represented in "Ktaadn, and the Maine Woods" and *Cape Cod.* Here "the Wild" finds its correlative in Thoreau's inward life ("[w]e have a wild savage in us"), and the "West" he explores is "symbolical of the path which we love to travel in the interior and ideal world." In this essay, "Life consists *with* wildness" (*W,* 5:224, 237, 217, 226; emphasis added in final quotation).

index
≈

Page numbers in italics refer to illustrations.